The Mahi Way

Choosing Right Over Popular

Building a lasting business centred around a vision-led, non-negotiable work culture

Mahijeet Mishra

With a foreword by Sekhar Seshan, Retd. Executive Editor, *Business India* Publications

Verses Kindler Publication

Verses Kindler Publication.
Website: www.verseskindlerpublication.com

The Mahi Way - Choosing Right Over Popular
By: Mr. **Mahijeet Mishra**
ISBN: 978-93-47494-61-1
1st Edition
Price: INR 299/$18

Disclaimer

The Mahi Way - Choosing Right Over Popular is authored by **Mahijeet Mishra**. The entirety of this published work comprises the original content of the author, who has undertaken diligent efforts in its editing. The characters depicted herein may be fictitious or inspired by real events; however, they are not intended to cause offense or represent any prejudice against any caste or system. Any similarity to the names of actual individuals, locations, or institutions is purely coincidental and serves the narrative. The author bears sole responsibility for the originality of this work; the publisher assumes no liability thereof.

Rashmi - Two and a half decades of riding together the roller coasters of life, little did we know we were creating memories for our weekend coffee conversations. Without you, I couldn't have pulled it off alone.

Manjari and Ramyani-everything I do is for you, and because of you.

Foreword

This was during my tenure as Executive Editor and Bureau Chief (South) for *Business India* magazine. A colleague had just returned from Chennai after visiting a three-shift operational manufacturing company, the Indian subsidiary of century-old Armstrong International Inc. She told me something extraordinary: nothing there was kept under lock. There were no surveillance cameras. No frisking. Not even a main gate. Everything, she said, was completely open.

It sounded inconceivable, especially in a manufacturing set-up of the corporate world. I decided to see it for myself.

"Welcome to our second home," said the person manning the entry of this gateless facility while ushering my cab to the parking lot. In the absence of any signage, I was wondering where the reception was, when the same person escorted me to the reception, where it was written in bold: "Director of First Impression."

"How was your entry experience at the main gate?" Managing Director, Mahijeet Mishra, asked mischievously when I was ushered into his office. I wasn't expecting a mid-thirties guy occupying the chair. I shared what I saw. There had been no entry process at all. No gate. Not under repair. Simply non-existent. No signage, too.

"Because you have none at home, either," said Mahijeet with a smile.

This, I learned, was the company's way of operating, rooted in an uncompromising belief in trust. Anyone could walk in: employee or visitor, known or unknown.

The same principle extended to the workers' pantry. There was no cash counter, only a large jar in which employees deposited the cost of whatever they consumed, reaching in to take back any change due.

As I spent more time walking through the facility and interacting with employees, my amazement only grew. Even the petty cash box with the accountant had no lock. There was no employee in-and-out time clock. No verbose policy manuals collecting dust. No travel policy. No multi-layered expense approval mechanisms. People spent money and claimed it without approval. No fashionable slogans adorned the walls. Just values.

I remember thinking then that it was one thing for founders in the US to conceptualise such a work culture, but quite another for a professional manager to live it and drive it forward, thousands of miles away, in India.

When asked how he had managed to build and sustain such a culture here, Mahijeet responded with characteristic humility. Living by core values, he said, is in his genes. And his stints across several companies had taught him what *not* to do as a business leader. By consciously avoiding those mistakes, he gradually built a unique enterprise, one distinguished not only by its unthinkable work culture but also by deep client loyalty, committed suppliers, engaged employees, and an impressive market share in what earlier had appeared to be a near-monopolistic market.

Mishra has summarized his corporate lessons and insights of three decades in this crisp and rich management book.

What I like about the book is that, although almost every paragraph is rich with management lessons, instead of writing it as a traditional management book, he has chosen to convey those as a story – a journey- making every page engaging, insightful, and relatable.

Rich with real-life case stories from his own journey, it stands out for its frankness, making this work, in many ways, autobiographical.

What makes Mahijeet's story compelling and enjoyable is not the idealism of his approach, but the honesty with which he recounts its challenges. I think this book is for those seeking to lead with purpose and create a business that lasts for generations.

I am happy to write this foreword for someone who has consistently chosen what is right over what is merely popular.

Sekhar Seshan

An Author & Journalist At Large

Acknowledgement

To my parents, Madhav Chandra and Abha, who grounded me in values that never bend. Like yours, those principles made the early years of my career tougher, and I stumbled more than I succeeded, but looking back, they built the kind of resilience that lasts.

To the friends, colleagues, former colleagues, and the many startup founders I've had the privilege to mentor: your growth gave me the courage to write this book. You showed me that my unconventional way of looking at business problems, often labelled "impractical", actually works. One of you even gave this approach its name: The *MahiWay*.

To Gus, David, Patrick, Doug, Kurt, and the entire Armstrong & Bloss family that I have worked with, thank you for steering Armstrong International Inc. with unwavering ethics for five generations. And thank you for giving me the freedom to practise ethical leadership in my own way; the *MahiWay*, earlier in establishing and shaping Armstrong in India, and now in leading Asia & Oceania.

To Rashmi, thank you for your patience every weekend over the past 11 months while I poured myself into writing the manuscript. I owe you a vacation.

And finally, to Tutor Scholastic, for helping me edit my thick manuscript, into this concise book.

Why this management book, when there are many?

First, my corporate journey stands on a long trail of failures and struggles. Those setbacks taught me far more than any success ever did. By sharing them - as someone who has been there, done that - I hope to make the path a little smoother for people who want to lead, *not by telling them what to do because that's unique with every individual, but by showing them the mistakes worth avoiding.*

Second, I have held tightly to my ethical values throughout my journey into corporate leadership. I thought the spirit of ethical leadership should be shared widely, to create workplaces where people feel safe, valued, respected, and free from biases that quietly erode belonging. *A workplace where self-induced pressure replaces the internal resistive stress.* Like the Mom of the family who always loads themselves with time-bound self-imposed work pressure but never without that 'signature smile'. I have come to believe that companies that let revenue lead workplace culture may grow fast, but only those that let revenue follow workplace culture truly go far.

And third, a more personal reason. For years, I felt out of place in forums where polished speakers used flawless English, diagrams, acronyms, and elaborate concepts to explain business decisions. I often walked away feeling inadequate instead of inspired. It took me decades to accept that my simple, jargon-free way of solving problems, clear enough for a seventh grader, actually works, and has worked consistently for my mentees and me. This book is my way of reaching others who feel the same sense of disconnect.

Preface

'MahiWay…'

From highway to subway, from expressway to freeway, and from the hard way or the shortcut way, we've heard of them all. Perhaps not this one.

MahiWay, which is the heart and soul of this book, is a way of leading, thinking, and growing.

I want to clarify something right at the outset: This is not the easiest way, or even the most direct, or the fastest one. But the most obvious one. People I work with find me as something of a Master of the Obvious, and so, naturally, the path that I follow and am trying to propagate is also rooted in what is evident.

Over the last three decades of working in department leadership and P&L leadership roles, across industries, teams, and geographies, I've often been asked: "How do you manage to lead with such clarity, even when things are uncertain?" or "How do you build culture, loyalty, and performance without micromanaging or pushing people to burnout?"

This book is my honest attempt to answer those questions.

And who am I?

My name is Mahijeet Mishra- the originator of the '*MahiWay*'.

I am currently President for Asia & Oceania at Armstrong International Inc., a global leader in thermal utilities and energy management for over 125 years.

I am blessed to have found my calling, and the work that I do gives me immense pleasure.

My experiences have shaped not just the business outcomes that I have been able to secure, but also the way I view leadership.

Going further back in time in my story, let me share something that might astound you as much as it astounds me to date!

If someone had told my younger self that one day I'd be writing a book on corporate leadership, I probably would've laughed, nervously, in broken English. Because neither confidence nor English came naturally to me.

I did my entire schooling in Kendriya Vidyalaya, where Hindi was the default language for everything that wasn't Mathematics or Science. I was bright, well-known in school, and even confident. Until suddenly, I wasn't.

Everything changed when a new student joined our class in Grade 10, coming from an English medium convent school. He was fluent in English, popular among the girls, and had no hesitation in making fun of my mustard-oiled hair or my Bihari accent.

Sitting next to him, I learned early that confidence could crumble when the world dictated what "smart" should look and sound like, equating a person's wisdom with their command of English.

It took me years to shake off that weight. But I did. Slowly, stubbornly. Not by learning perfect grammar, but by finding my voice.

I carried that resolve into the Rural Engineering College, where I studied. There, I found the stage, and I could spread my wings. I participated in every debate and extempore competition I could find, forcing myself to speak, to improve, to organise my thoughts.

By the end of my degree, I hadn't become an orator, but I'd become something far more powerful: comfortable in my own skin. It became my biggest asset.

The introvert had now become an ambivert, ready to get launched in the corporate world.

Between my graduation in 1995 and my interview at Armstrong International in 2009, I had already worked with six companies, never leaving one for money or for title.

Each role taught me something. Each decision shaped me. But Armstrong gave me something different; it gave me space. Freedom. And responsibility. I was asked to build something in India that didn't exist here: a Sales & Operations set-up, a company culture based on absolute trust, with no gates, no surveillance cameras, and no dirt-eating policy manuals. Just values.

And while others may have seen that as an idealistic theory, I took the challenge as it resonated with my personality.

Over time, for Armstrong's start-up venture in India, I've had to build teams, open markets, deal with monopolies, defend ethics when it wasn't popular, and say "no" when everyone wanted a convenient "yes." There were no manuals to rely on or any instructions that told me how to go about this mammoth task.

Adding to the challenge, this unique culture had to be established in Chennai, where I couldn't communicate with most of my team due to my limited command of the local language.

I had to figure out a way for myself. But values became my compass. And they never let me go astray.

Watching this venture earn a strong market share, something that once felt out of reach in the early years, has only reinforced my belief that businesses can thrive for the long haul when they're rooted in core values. Doing the right thing, even when it's not fashionable, builds a foundation that lasts.

That's the essence of the *MahiWay*- an ethical and morally strong approach that helps in navigating every situation that a workplace will ever throw at you. And it works, as it did for me.

All the stories and scenarios in this book are real, and every action described is something I've lived and practised for years, before putting across to you.

However, to keep the narration simple and protect identities, I've used fictional company name and characters.

Let me introduce you to the protagonist, Mr. Prithvi Kashyap.

Like any seasoned leader, Prithvi has faced moments of doubt, stretches of uncertainty, and situations where the right path was also the harder one. But he has a way of taking each challenge, breaking it down, and finding a way through without losing sight of what matters most.

In the sections ahead, you will walk alongside Prithvi as he tackles situations that will feel familiar, no matter where you are in your career.

If you are an entrepreneur trying to grow something in a competitive market, you will find echoes of your own struggles here. If you are in mid to senior management, managing teams, meeting targets, and balancing conflicting priorities, you will recognise the weight of the choices he has to make. And if you are someone who wants to lead with purpose, you will see how such leadership looks not in theory, but in practice.

In a world where it is easy to compromise in the name of speed or convenience, I hope his experiences remind you that there is another way. A way that holds on to integrity without letting go of results. A way that values people as much as performance.

That way, as you will see, is what I call the *MahiWay*. And I believe that once you see it in action through Prithvi's story, you might just find pieces of it becoming part of your own journey too.

Meet Prithvi Kashyap

Prithvi Kashyap is the kind of man you cannot miss in a room. Not because he towers over others; with his 5-foot-11-inch height, he does not have an overbearing frame.

But what lends him an unmissable trait is the sheer presence he exerts and the way he commands attention, without ever asking for it.

His personality is immensely pleasing. His eyes have a special tendency to always look razor-sharp and yet reflect immense kindness, too.

Prithvi comes from an Indian middle-class, Hindi-speaking family, the kind where youngsters were taught never to counter elders, interrupting them was unthinkable, to be home before the streetlights came on, watching TV meant watching Doordarshan news, and violating any core value often meant standing outside the house for long hours. One tight slap from Dad was considered a course correction, not an act of child abuse.

He did his schooling at a school where Hindi was the default language.

He is the quintessential Family Man. Along with the professional accolades he holds, he also thoroughly enjoys being a husband and a father.

His wife, Kiran, is a homemaker who chose to focus entirely on their family and devote herself to raising their two daughters. The results are evident: their elder daughter, Manvi, completed her bachelor's in mechanical engineering from a premier institute and now works with a global food giant in the Europe zone, while their younger daughter, Soumya, is pursuing her bachelor's in medicine, MBBS, from one of India's top medical universities.

Coming to his professional life, Prithvi is the appointed Managing Director of Bloam International, a global premium industrial machinery conglomerate.

He has always been the epitome of unshakeable values, sincerity, and discipline, consistently determined to give his best and work hard. He lives by the belief that the harder you work, the smarter you become, and hence luckier.

So naturally, it seems like an obvious story, doesn't it?

A bright student climbs steadily up the corporate ladder until one day, at the age of 35, he's sitting in the Managing Director's chair.

Except, Prithvi's story was nothing like that.

Because if you think it was all neat and predictable, you're in for a surprise. His rise wasn't a straight upward line at all.

It had its bumps, its detours, and a few unexpected turns that shaped him into the leader he eventually became.

Almost two decades ago, Prithvi had walked into the lavish offices of Bloam International for his interview for the position of Sales & Marketing Director, as they were planning to establish their presence in the Indian market.

The interviewer, an executive committee member with years of experience sizing up candidates, had his resume printed and ready on the table. After exchanging pleasantries, he got straight to the point, the burning issue that would undoubtedly cross anyone's mind upon looking at Prithvi's career record.

"Your educational qualifications are impressive, no doubt. But what concerns me is that you seem to have a lot of problems staying put at a job. Your resume looks like that of an impulsive job hopper; never content to stay in one place for the long term."

Most people would have defended themselves nervously, maybe tried to laugh it off. But Prithvi looked straight into the eyes and said, his voice steady:

"If fourteen years of surviving through suffocation and mental agony every single day sounds impulsive or like a job-hopper, then be it. My wife and I know what we've gone through, those years of being part of filthy office politics, bad-isms, biases, character assassination for failing to ego-massage the bosses, and dirty games played on someone coming from a humble background and talks straight, as I, someone who asks for nothing but sense in what he is doing. If quitting jobs in the simple expectation of doing the right thing is impulsive, then I am okay with being called impulsive.

But let me also tell you this: When a man who is the sole bread earner of his family quits without another job in hand, it doesn't show instability. It shows how much he values his ethics and peace of mind above everything else."

The interviewer was astounded. He had expected excuses, maybe a defensive ramble. Instead, here was a man who did not flinch while admitting his choices.

Prithvi's tone and demeanour remained calm and almost disarmingly candid. For a moment, the interviewer forgot about the resume. He leaned back in his chair, studying Prithvi's face.

"Tell me your story," he said quietly.

And Prithvi began.

"My first job was right after I completed engineering, and it seemed perfect," Prithvi explained. I was promoted three times in a year and a half. At twenty-two, I was already Shift In-charge, leading a small team. We were responsible for crude oil extraction and dispatch to refineries. I worked hard, earned respect, and for the first time felt the thrill of leadership. Till I was confronted with the reality of my company..."

Taking a pause, Prithvi continued, "It was owned by someone who was on a two-year sabbatical from his company. He had bought the oil wells with the intent to sell them after his paid leave ended.

I found it extremely unethical; we were all working hard to build something, but it was never meant to last. It was a channel to pass the time and earn profits; it was never about creating value or an honest business.

It did not sit right with me. It did not make sense to me, and so, I would not do it.

I put in my papers and left the job, learning the management lesson that

A founder without a vision and an employee with a vision can't coexist.

After a round of applications and interviews, I landed my second job."

As he narrated his story, there was never hesitation in Prithvi's tone. He never once fumbled, tried to overtly justify his actions, or seek validation about whether he was right. The clarity and honesty were refreshing.

"I was a Project Engineer in a company handling Food & Beverage greenfield projects. Those 3.9 years I spent gave me great exposure; I travelled across India installing green and brown field plants, and I completed a record-breaking thirteen projects for different clients in that time. One of our client projects involved expanding an existing beverage plant into what was set to become the largest in Asia. One day, while passing through the existing plant with my electrician, I noticed something odd in the facility. Long rows of workers sat on stools beside the sachet dispensers, collecting sachets as they fell from the machines and neatly arranging them in crates for cold storage. It struck me as a huge waste of people's time and talent for a task that could easily be automated.

We already had similar machines lying in our site warehouse to be installed for the capacity expansion project. So, we quietly pulled one out of its carton, set it aside, drew a curtain around our little corner, and began what we jokingly started calling our "secret mission."

One month later, we had successfully managed to modify that machine into a fully automated system.

When the client's director learned of our innovation, he wholeheartedly acknowledged that our effort would improve efficiency and could reduce labour by half, allowing it to be redeployed to more labour-intensive work. He also praised the initiative while sharing the innovation with our Managing Director.

However, our MD responded in a radically different way. 'How much company money did you spend?' he asked. He first asked us how much money we had spent. We truthfully answered that since it was all from scrap, we had spent almost nothing.

Next, he inquired who had asked us to do it. I confessed that it was merely a result of my curiosity about whether the process could be improved since the current practice made no sense to me.

I remember so vividly what he said to me after that- "Next time, talk to your manager before you try to satisfy your curiosity.' I was stunned.

A week later, the company received its biggest ever order, to modify and automate all the machines. Yet, not a single word of recognition came from the Managing Director. It's important to clarify something here," Prithvi added, leaning ahead. "I wasn't praise-hungry. But I could not stand being chastised for simply taking a good initiative and not getting my due respect."

With a small smile, Prithvi continued, "It was a very tough decision. I was two years married, and my wife was seven months pregnant at the time. Besides, I was still bound by a four-year contract, and quitting three months before the end meant paying a massive penalty.

I emptied our savings, borrowed from a college friend, and still barely scraped the amount. It cost a lot to get myself out of there, but the way I think of it, it was the price of my work ethic and integrity. It was one I was willing to bear."

I left the company having learned a set of management lessons:

Never put profit above people.

Treat others the way you want to get treated. And,

A company should never take for granted its aligned & performing members, as they are generally more vulnerable.

Otherwise, the company may find themself deputing four project managers to fill the void left by the departure of just one."

The interviewer thought for a second about how he, himself, would react in similar situations. The motivations for leaving were clear, but were they big enough to actually take that leap and quit? Couldn't the candidate wait for three more months to prevent emptying the entire bank savings?

But before he thought about it any further, the interviewer realised something and smiled. It did not matter what he thought; it was clear that for Prithvi, the reasons were big enough, and nothing could convince him otherwise. Here was a man who knew exactly what he stood for.

"My third job was a completely different role in B2B valve sales", Prithvi continued. "Since I had no prior sales experience, they took me in at the entry-level wage and entry-level job title, despite having five years of work experience by then. I didn't mind because I was willing to start fresh and learn. But I had to learn all the things that I never wanted to know about.

For the four years that I worked there, each day was marked by my cooking up lies for clients. Never because I wanted to, but because I had to. We lied about shipments, about documentation, about product performance. There was a clear directive from my reporting manager to get as many sales as possible, even if it entailed unethical practices.

To top it all, the Head of Sales, an alumnus of one of India's top engineering institutes, had no field sales experience whatsoever. His educational background and mastery of dashboard creation earned him his rank. However, his authoritative leadership style and textbook-driven expectations fostered a culture of fear across the entire sales organization, down to the grassroots level at which I worked.

Fear gave rise to hiding facts and then to dishonesty. Lacking real sales experience and being elevated straight to the *you do-I watch* level, he was unable to sense such happenings. Unchecked, they eventually led to a culture of bigger unethical practices.

The structure of the company itself was also flawed. Department Leaderships were divided between the South India team and the Western India management, and each side pulled in a different direction, thereby leading to biases and bad-isms. Favouritism, casteism, regionalism, you name it, and it was practised there. I belonged to none of those camps, nor did I have any Godfather to sort things out for me. The chairman was a humble and caring individual, but had chosen to remain oblivious, maybe since sales were pouring in.

I was on my own. I stuck it out for as long as I did because I had family responsibilities. But the culture, or lack thereof, eventually got to a point where it became unbearably suffocating.

I did not see any sense in the way the business was being run. And so, I did not see any sense in continuing there.

I left the company having learned several management lessons:

When focus on short-term revenue growth overshadows long-term cultural alignment, we invite others to take away portions of our market share-slowly but surely.

Biases are cancerous- they spread faster than we think they would.

Grassroot-level work experience is a must to evolve as a visionary leader.

To build a cohesive & convergent team, focus more on the healing you provide than on the harm you can cause. And,

A good company led by a great human being is, ultimately, only as good as its people. While revenue may rise from the bottom up, culture must travel top down."

Counting off each experience on his fingers, Prithvi continued, "Coming to job number 4 now, in a Service Department. It was a major Indian brand, publicly listed, and had promoted itself as winner of the 'recommended place to work' award.

By this time, my resume had become an unusual mix: crude oil production, Food & Beverage projects, B2B sales, and now services. Each switch meant scaling down wages and titles, but I had made my peace with that.

First days in a new company always bring something new, but what I experienced was completely unexpected and rather horrifying.

The Human Resources representative walked me to what was going to be my office. But there was already a person occupying the office. Before I could express my confusion, the Human Resources executive told the man that he had been moved to another profile and that I was here to replace him.

I was as shocked as the other man. If this was their definition of professionalism, where he hadn't even been given the prior courtesy of being informed about the replacement, I didn't know what to expect.

Still, I tried to adjust and make it work. I embraced my role, but there was yet another shocker waiting for me. I discovered that my service-sales team didn't even have laptops, so they were spending more time at the office than at client premises. When I brought this up with my reporting manager, I was told that the requisition sent to Head Office three months ago was still awaiting approval.

I tried to make him see the reality that by the time approval would crawl its way through headquarters, an entire quarter would be wasted, and it would affect the annual sales target to be achieved. I couldn't understand why no one was accountable and why there was such a long wait for a basic requirement.

I spent the next month running from department to department trying to secure multi-layered approvals through. But it was like banging my head against a wall of red tape.

That was not what I wanted to spend my days doing. The way out seemed like the only way ahead for me.

So, I left the job without having another job in hand, with a couple of management lessons:

The longer the process, the costlier the output-if it is a process, it has to be lean.

Build a culture of transparency and fearlessness where even people getting replaced see it coming."

The interviewer sat back, stunned again. Four jobs, four exits. This wasn't a man who couldn't hold a job. This was a man who refused to sell his conscience for one.

And that made him very different from anyone the interviewer had ever met in his life!

"What happened at the fifth job?" he asked, curiosity getting the better of him.

"Let me tell you a bit about what happened before the fifth job came my way," Prithvi said with a smile.

"My wife has always been my rock, and, when needed, my strongest critic. During that phase of my life, she sat me down and told me that I would always have her support in standing by my values and ethics. But she also reminded me that values alone are not enough without growth.

"If your principles matter so deeply to you that you keep walking away from roles that don't align with them," she said, "then you need to place yourself where you have the power to make decisions."

She made me realize that by remaining in entry-level positions and switching jobs, I would never truly rise through the ranks to bring about the change I wanted to see. Those words became my turning point and my inspiration to prepare for one of the toughest entrance exams in the country: CAT.

I went on to crack it and eventually earned admission to one of India's most prestigious institutions, the Indian Institute of

Management (IIM), to pursue a postgraduate degree in business management.

Now, as an IIM graduate, I was brought in as General Manager to revive a company that was on the verge of collapse. I had no time for trial-and-error. I had to make decisions quickly, some easy, some hard, but all sensible.

In just one year, I transformed it into a double-digit operating profit company and created a solid team spread across the country. I had a great run there, for around one and a half years, and then something happened."

Shaking his head, almost as if the incident still disappoints him, he continued, "It was one month after the end of the fiscal year; a year in which we had earned hefty profits.

Then one morning, some of my team members worriedly told me that they hadn't received their wages for the month. I immediately approached Human Resources and was told of a 'fund crunch'. I couldn't accept that reasoning, and so, I went to the owner directly.

Truth was, our hard-earned profits had been siphoned off by him into another new venture that had gone bankrupt. What hurt me most was that he did this without informing anyone in the leadership team. And he had no better plans for revival either. I found this act of his unprofessional.

And so I resigned, again with a couple of lessons:

As a business owner, the moment you hire someone in your company, it no longer remains your company; it becomes our company. And,

The first thing that should go into the trash every morning is the ego."

Tapping at the resume on the table, the interviewer pointed at one name in particular. "This company is so reputable; Multinational Company and is a listed one too. I can't believe there are problems with culture or processes here!"

Prithvi simply said, "There weren't; not directly anyway. But eventually, a company is what it is made into by its leadership. And here, that was the biggest problem."

Letting his words sink in for a few minutes, he then continued, "Our local Managing Director was, for lack of a better word-spineless. He bent whichever way the wind blew. In every core committee meeting, I would see him lean towards the General Manager-Sales, even when the rest of us had data and arguments to prove otherwise.

Every day was a carousel of meetings. Meeting after meeting, discussion after discussion, and yet no real decisions. Plus, whenever conflicts arose, the Managing Director would simply smile and say: 'Yes, you are right. You are also right. Even you are right.'

It was frustrating. Leadership isn't about pleasing everyone. It's about taking a stand, even if it makes some people unhappy.

This went on for a while, and I finally asked myself: Do I really want to spend years under a leader who cannot take a firm stand? Is there any growth for me in this environment?

The clear answer to both questions was no. So, I walked away once again, like I did multiple times before, again by learning management lessons:

Take a stand. Period.

Never play favourites.

When you call a meeting, always calculate the cost of an hour spent multiplied by the wages of each invitee and make sure the 'return on meeting' is much larger.

But I have no regrets because each time, I walked out with something priceless intact: my ethics, my hard-earned experiences of things a company shouldn't be doing to continue thriving, and my peace of mind."

For several seconds after Prithvi had narrated his entire story, nobody spoke.

Then, the interviewer said quietly, "Mr Kashyap, in all my years of meeting candidates, I've heard people talk about success, ambition, strategy.

But never about suffocation. Never about the cost of integrity. You've walked away from more than most people would ever dare. And yet, here you sit, steady, unshaken."

It was clear in that instant that this was no longer an interview. It was a turning point.

To understand Prithvi's thinking, the interviewer asked, "Mr. Kashyap, we're the global leader in our industry and are preparing to enter the Indian market. If we put you in charge of this new venture, what kind of company would you build?"

Drawing from his experiences, Prithvi began outlining his thoughts, counting on his fingers as he spoke.

"First, I call it DNA mapping-not in literal terms but in thoughts & actions. I'd check whether the Vision statement of the company matches well with the founder's DNA because I have worked with companies wherein business owners turned a blind eye to their vision statement while steering the company towards a completely divergent path. In such cases, the vision statement ended up as nothing more than a photo frame hanging behind the receptionist.

Next would be mapping my personality with the company's vision and the founder's DNA. If the three don't meet, the partnership won't last. I've learned that the hard way.

Then I'd look at cash flow expectations and the company's risk appetite. That tells us whether we should begin big and absorb early losses or start small and scale steadily while staying profitable.

Next, I'd study the market, the voice of the market, unmet needs, and how these compare with our purpose. From there, a year-on-year business strategy will fall into place.

Based on that direction, I'd build a team of people, again with a DNA match.

The idea is to create a visionary company having a workplace free of the usual biases, a culture rooted in trust, clarity of purpose, and doing what's right even when it's not the popular choice."

The interviewer leaned back. "All of this sounds good, but isn't it a little too idealistic?"

Prithvi smiled. *"I look at it this way. Most of us are already successful CEOs at home. Even during economic recessions, when companies collapse, I rarely see their employees go bankrupt. They've saved well, planned well, and managed their households with discipline. So how does a group of such capable 'home-CEOs' come together at work and still end up sinking a company?"*

He paused and added, *"There isn't a single function at work that doesn't exist at home. We budget, plan, produce, negotiate, save, invest, and take responsibility. If we practise these principles in our personal lives, moreover, without any formal education on any of these, why can't we carry them into the workplace? The problem is only in the mindset; people treat home and work like two separate worlds. And if you ask me, they have been made to think this way because of the way they get treated at work. Companies reap what they sow."*

The interviewer didn't have a comeback.

"As you know, your interview today was for the position of Sales & Marketing Director. But, after having interacted with you, I don't believe we can ever find a better Managing Director than you for establishing and leading the company in India. Would you be interested in taking up that position?"

Prithvi gave a soft smile and said, "I had already told the placement agency, who seem to have failed to convey my message to you, that I was set to join another company as a Business Unit Manager the following week. I still came for this interview because your organisation has always been a dream workplace for me, and a part of me wanted to see if I should take that chance on myself. I am grateful for the offer, but I respectfully have to decline it. My ethics permitted me to come up to your doorstep today, but they will not permit me to step over that threshold. I have to uphold the commitment I have already made."

A candidate dropping an offer for the Managing Director of his dream company to choose a Business Unit Manager position was unheard of. But, by then, the interviewer was well aware of the fact that a moral compass as strong as Prithvi Kashyap's was also unheard of!

He asked for every detail of the work Prithvi was to undertake in the other company and asked Prithvi how long he would take to complete it.

"I am confident that I will be able to complete what I am required to do there in a period of one year," Prithvi answered.

"Okay, then," the interviewer said with a smile. "We will have you on board after a year. Until then, we will fill up other positions, including the one you just vacated, of Sales & Marketing Director". Both laughed.

"Only if I am allowed not to do what doesn't make sense.", said Prithvi with a curt smile.

The interviewer held his gaze. Then, slowly, he extended his hand. "You'll have it."

Fast forward to 365 days later. As predicted by Prithvi, he had accomplished his mission with the other company.

That same day, an email arrived in his inbox, and by the next morning, he found himself in Bloam International's lavish office again.

"The seat of the Managing Director is waiting for you," the interviewer told him with a smile. "Are you ready for it now?"

"I am," Prithvi said with a smile.

And with that handshake, Prithvi Kashyap stepped into the role that would one day define him, not as another cog in the corporate wheel, but as a man determined to prove that integrity and leadership were not opposites.

They could, and must, exist together.

From 21, when he first stepped into the corporate world, to 31, when he was still at entry-level wages and titles, and now at 35, as Managing Director of a global leader in industrial machinery, he carried the weight of past experiences, along with mixed emotions:

certain of the workplace culture he wanted to build, yet uncertain because such a culture had never existed before.

But the one person who stood certain was Kiran.

Story 1: Compassion is the Strongest Command

The move to Karnataka did not come to Prithvi as a sudden break in his career but as another bend in a road that had long been winding. By then, turbulence had become familiar to him.

But those moments of hardship carved something deeper in him. They hardened him, yes, but they also softened him. They gave him compassion, the kind that does not come from theories or books but from knowing what it is to explain to your family why you have chosen principle over comfort, and to live through the strain of that choice.

By the time he was preparing to assume his new responsibilities in Karnataka, compassion was no longer just one virtue among many to him. It had become his compass. He had also come to embrace a conviction that gave shape to everything he did as a leader: leadership was not unlike parenting. In fact, he would say, parenting was harder. No one trained parents, no manual was handed to them, yet most managed to raise children who were loved, safe, and whole.

They fed, guided, disciplined, and most importantly, believed in their children. If that could be done at home, why not in the workplace? For Prithvi, the two worlds were not separate; they were mirrors of each other. Running a company, he insisted, was no different from running a home. If a home was built on trust, love, and responsibility, then so too must an organisation be.

That conviction was already set when he first reported not to Karnataka but to a rented space in Chennai, where operations had been temporarily housed while the new plant was still being built. Before Prithvi joined, twenty-two people had already joined the company eight months earlier. He never forgot the memory of that first morning.

He was led through a hall where there were cubes, and people were bent over their monitors, and not a single pair of eyes dared to look out.

He was followed by silence like a shadow. There was no laughter, no chatter, just the stillness of people uncertain how to behave around a new boss. The HR manager finally deposited him in a large corner office, a polished Managing Director's chamber with a heavy desk, a nameplate, and a door that shut him away from everyone else. The room was less an office than a wall.

He lasted only a few minutes inside. Then he called the HR manager back and asked for a free cubicle, preferably in the middle of the floor. The man looked stunned, but Prithvi was firm. Within the hour, he was seated among the staff, not above them. The unease around him was palpable. Employees fidgeted, glanced sideways, whispered under their breath. A Managing Director, among them, was as foreign a sight as if a headmaster had decided to sit in a school classroom among the students.

The tension stretched till lunchtime, when he made his second move. He declared a half-day off. However, rather than letting everyone leave for home, he sent everyone to a recreation session for the rest of the day. Their only assignment was to know each other well, to the extent that they could tell everything about each other's families.

The next day was a test for everyone. Rather than having lunch by himself or allowing anyone to have lunch by themselves at their desks like they always did, he invited everyone to take their lunch boxes into the big office and eat together at the big table. They reluctantly obeyed, hauling their *dabbas* with a combination of suspicion and curiosity. Sitting down, they sat in silence, not knowing what was to be done.

Prithvi disrupted the ritual with a simple experiment. Instead of inviting each to introduce themselves, he invited them to introduce the person sitting beside them, knowing well that normally people sit next to those they are most comfortable with. The exercise was part-joke, part-test, and its outcome was telling: embarrassment, laughter, and the self-conscious realisation of how little they knew about each other beyond job title, even when they were given half a day to spend with one another. Few could mention the first name of a colleague's spouse or the number of children they had.

Prithvi seized the moment. If they were going to work like a family, he told them, then they had to know each other like a family, not just as job roles but as people. At home, relationships were not built on résumés but on familiarity and care. Work had to be the same.

The ice broke, not only between them and their new boss but among themselves.

That was the beginning of what would become his style: dismantling the distance that formality imposed, turning the workplace into something that felt closer to a home. Over the following weeks, he reinforced the message in ways that were simple but powerful. He began to chip away at the idea that office hours were rigid boundaries.

"Do you ever tell your children to study exactly eight hours a day?" he would ask.

"Not one hour more, not one less? No. You want them to learn, to grow, to stay curious. You measure not the minutes but the outcome." He wanted them to see that work, too, should not be measured in clocked hours but in commitment, alignment, togetherness, outcome, and ownership.

For some, this was liberating. For others, unsettling. They were used to thinking that arriving on time and staying late equalled dedication. This new approach demanded responsibility of a different sort; it asked them to integrate their work and their lives instead of splitting themselves into two people: the one from eight to six and the one after six. He told them openly, "You are not two different people. If you are honest and responsible at home, bring that honesty and responsibility here. Be one person, not two."

He backed his words with his actions. He told his staff again and again, "I will take care of you the way I take care of my daughters. Your career growth, your safety, and your family's well-being, I will carry these as my responsibility. In return, I only ask you to give yourself fully to this organisation without expecting about what you get in return." Many were stunned to hear such words from a boss. Some resisted, doubting it could be true. Some took it as a stunt to extract more work. Some took it as a subtle hint of wafer-thin wage rise. But slowly, trust began to take root.

One of the first tests of this trust came when he was informed by HR of a young employee browsing job sites during office hours. The HR saw this as violation of work ethics hence had complained to Prithvi. He was surprised; he thought the man was happy. Instead of reprimanding him, Prithvi invited him in for a conversation. Instead of raising an objection to browsing job sites during work hours, Prithvi asked gently why he was looking elsewhere. The young man hesitated, then admitted he was about to get married and feared his salary would not be enough. Prithvi asked why he had not spoken to him. The man replied, "Sir, you once told us those who ask will never get. I thought it meant I should never share my needs."

Prithvi smiled sadly. "I said those who expect will not get. I did not mean you cannot share your problems. A mother and child never expect anything from each other, but they share everything. Maybe I should have said it differently."

He then gave him a sheet of paper and asked him if he is willing to write down every expense he had. Hesitating initially at an MD asking to write down all the personal expenses, he wrote down all.

As Prithvi studied it, he realised the man was also sending money to his sister, who was trapped in a difficult marriage, and that he was putting his savings into chit funds that were risky. He shook his head. "You need savings, not just a higher salary." He raised the man's wages substantially, making sure at least twenty per cent was forced into safe savings each month. He guided him to close the chit funds, to open accounts in nationalised banks, and to start a Public Provident Fund account. He arranged vocational training for his sister so she could earn a living for herself. What might have been a resignation turned into loyalty, gratitude, and stability. Years later, that same young employee went on to head the same department and lead a team of twenty.

The HR manager wasn't pleased about raising an employee's salary midway through the financial year. He approached Prithvi and said, "This might send the wrong signal. What if others start asking for the same?"

Prithvi replied, "I appreciate your concern. It shows you care about the organisation. I've been observing this employee closely. He works hard, needs no reminders, delivers results, and is fully aligned with our culture. He was honest about his financial troubles. If he were my son, I'd have done exactly what I did today. And let's do the same for anyone who shows the same level of cultural alignment delivering result consistently without any reminder.

A team is only as strong as its weakest member. I simply strengthened ours."

The HR manager got his first Prithvi lesson.

The story spread quickly through the company, not as gossip but as proof that when he said he would care for them like family, he meant it. People also started to realise that they can see their wages & career grow if they perform, behave, and act with the same level of ownership and commitment the way they do in their personal life.

Gradually, stories like this began to change how the staff saw him. They no longer described him in the language of corporate hierarchy. They said, "He takes care of us like his own children." It was not rhetoric. It was their lived experience. And in return, their energy and loyalty deepened.

For Prithvi, the point was never about lowering attrition numbers or creating incentive plans. It was about creating a place where people felt they belonged, where they were seen and heard, where they did not need to put on a different mask to come to work. He believed rules and policies could force compliance but never inspire commitment. Only trust could do that. Only compassion could do that.

Another initiative was to challenge one of the most entrenched practices of all, the employee in-and-out time clock. Such approaches bred mistrust. He rejected them outright. "Do you ever tell your daughter she will only get your love if she studies an extra hour?" he asked them.

"No. You celebrate her effort and her result, not the clock." The message was clear: they would not measure work in extra hours or exact hours but in the value created. If someone stayed late for an urgent shipment, it was ownership. If someone left early for family, it was also ownership. One balanced the other in a culture of trust. He demonstrated it himself, once asking the team to accelerate a shipment so that they could all leave two hours early and reclaim their day as people, not just workers.

At first, some were uneasy. Those from stricter backgrounds wondered whether their work would be recognised if it wasn't tied to visible sacrifices of time. Others abused the freedom, mistaking it for license. But Prithvi dealt with both as a parent would, with firmness when necessary, gentleness when possible, but always fairness. He reminded them that in a family, there is freedom, but not without responsibility. Parents don't watch every step, but they intervene when harm appears. Slowly, the team learned.

It was a surprise for everyone when the shopfloor team came forward, voluntarily forgoing their overtime hours to match with others in the company. As the time-clock concept vanished, it was replaced by a natural rhythm of working when necessary and resting when necessary.

People once found it hilarious when Prithvi sponsored cinema tickets to a newlywed employee who had asked Prithvi permission to leave early since his wife was feeling romantic to go movie together. Prithvi had said, "You chose to be honest and fearless instead of giving a lame excuse of having a headache as a reason for leaving early. Your honesty has earned you the movie tickets from me."

Even more radical was the locked cash box maintained by the Finance executive. Prithvi had to make this also lock-free.

"At home, children know where the money is kept. They know where jewellery is. But generally, they don't steal, because trust and transparency make stealing impossible." Said, Prithvi.

So, he asked the Finance executive to remove the lock from the cash box, so a culture of mutual trust could be built across the organisation.

Another similar cash box was for the pantry.

"At home," he would say, "you don't ask your child to sign a receipt when they take ten rupees to buy snacks. They know where the wallet cupboard is. They take, they use, and they return with change. Sometimes they forget the change, but you never stop trusting them. Sometimes, they refuse the change. That is when you get an opportunity to align them to your family culture. Why? Because trust is what makes a home possible."

So, one morning, he asked the administration team to put a small wooden cash box beside every pantry rack across the facility. People had to simply drop cash as per the price mentioned on the item they were picking. There was no lock, no register, no surveillance, no monitoring. The reaction was disbelief. Employees whispered that it was a trap, some sort of test.

Critics called it reckless. What if someone misused it? His reply was steady: "If we can't trust our people with money, the fault is not with them but with the culture we have built."

He added, "If we can trust our people with machinery and inventories worth millions on the shop floor, we can certainly trust them with a petty cash box or pantry supplies. There shouldn't be a single lock anywhere in the organisation. We shouldn't compromise on what's right just because it comes with a few challenges."

He went on, "And about misuse, I believe, the number of people who might take advantage will always be tiny compared to those who live by our values. Companies are built by and for culturally aligned people. Let's focus on them, and not on the exceptions."

Prithvi was right. Because of the trust placed in them, very few people stole. Even fewer cheated. And when someone did cross the line, Prithvi made it clear to HR not to waste time hunting for defaulters.

Instead, he communicated a clear message across the company: "continued cheating or stealing signalled a rejection of the culture of trust, and a preference to be treated like employees rather than as members of the family."

People understood the unspoken message behind Prithvi's words. They noticed that while other companies ran fixed bus routes for employee pick & drop, Prithvi ensured every employee was picked up from their doorstep, even at a significantly higher cost to the company. While others provided non-air-conditioned buses even during summer's scorching heat to their employees, Prithvi made sure everyone travelled in air-conditioned comfort. Where most companies monitored work hours, Prithvi chose not to.

They knew they would lose the 'family' treatment if they acted only like employees.

The results were visible almost immediately. People aligned, not because they were watched, but because they were trusted.

Still, there were a few tempted ones who continued to steal and were quietly shown the door, not because of the money, but because they were not meant to stay.

The box became more than just a place for cash; it became a symbol, whispered about to new recruits, pointed out as proof that the company was different.

Over the next few weeks, the same approach was applied on the shop floor. The inventory manager role was removed, and the long chain of requisition slips disappeared. Machine Operators were empowered to pick materials directly from the racks and simply log their entries into the ERP system. The steady rise in inventory accuracy proved that the culture was working.

This same philosophy ran through his approach to employee retention.

He reimagined it entirely.

Shruti, his newly appointed HR Manager, once recalled an early experience that stayed with her.

"In my first few weeks, I was eager to impress the leadership. At my previous organization, I had been praised for designing employee retention strategies, so I sent Prithvi a calendar invite for an hour-long meeting titled 'Employee Retention Policy Discussion.'

Within a minute, he was at my desk. He said, 'Shruti, when you prepare for this meeting, only talk about the things you do at home to retain your son from leaving you."

She laughed as she added, "I realized I had to rethink the whole invite. At home, we don't 'retain' family. We give love, care, and affection selflessly. Retention just happens naturally."

Where other firms drafted heavy contracts, imposed notice periods, or bound employees with bonds, especially before deputing them for an overseas project, he found such practices absurd.

"Would you ever chain your child to the house to stop them from leaving?" he asked one senior manager.

"No. You make the house so full of warmth, so safe, so loving, that they don't want to leave. That is how it should be here. Not by compulsion, but by choice."

On another occasion, an HR manager from the same industrial township approached Prithvi with a proposal.

"We're planning to introduce a 'no-poaching' agreement among companies in the township," he said. "No firm would hire employees from another. Would your company like to join?"

Prithvi paused and replied calmly, "Would you make the same agreement with your neighbors to stop them from taking your son? Or, in your words, 'poaching' your son?"

The HR manager left shortly after, slightly embarrassed.

Prithvi refused to believe in golden handcuffs. Instead, he created golden bridges, reasons to stay that were built on care, not contracts. He invested in families, not just individuals.

Another initiative that Prithvi implemented, which attracted commendation from families, was to declare an extra paid holiday on the 'marriage anniversary'. This initiative, too, came from a lived experience.

He learnt that one young energy manager worked so hard that he missed his own wedding anniversary two years in a row. His wife never complained, never told Prithvi, but someone else mentioned it in passing. Prithvi called the man in, looked him in the eye, and told him he was changing his annual performance bonus letter. The letter that year read: "To claim this half a million-rupee bonus, you must spend at least three nights and four days at a luxury resort abroad with your family, with your office phone switched off. If you violate any clause, you forfeit the bonus." The employee was stunned, then grateful, and his wife, years later, still told people that it was the best gift her husband had ever brought home.

The outcomes were unexpected.

This spirit even extended to how he viewed clients and suppliers. He often repeated what became his ethical cornerstone: *"Treat your suppliers and clients like a spouse, and your employees like your children."* A spouse, he said, is not someone you exploit but someone you respect, with whom you keep promises even when times are hard. A child is not someone you love conditionally, only when convenient, but someone you care for unconditionally.

The metaphor might have sounded strange, but people who worked with him found it made everything simple. It stripped away jargon about stakeholders and replaced it with human relationships.

His conviction about one life also dictated how he dealt with generational differences among the employees. It was, perhaps, the most telling proof of his approach.

The older employees, seasoned in rigid cultures, expected aloof, autocratic leadership. The younger ones demanded freedom and flexibility. Instead of forcing both into one mould, he handled them as a parent handles children of different ages. To the seniors, he gave respect and patience, asking them to teach and honouring their experience while gently introducing change.

To the juniors, he gave freedom but demanded accountability, letting them experiment but guiding them back when needed. It was not easy, but it worked because it was sincere. Each felt they were treated justly, each according to their need, like children in a family.

His approach was clearly visible at the Karnataka plant, which attracted workers from various backgrounds, fresh recruits who were hungry for liberty, middle-aged workers moulded by more austere companies, and older workers who had spent their working lives in fixed hierarchies. They all wanted a different type of leadership. The young ones resented too much control, demanding flexibility and experimentation. The old ones felt uncomfortable without rules and structure, demanding clear lines of control.

Instead of compelling one side to be different, Prithvi handled them like a parent handles children of varying ages. To the younger ones, he left space to experiment, to ask questions, to play with concepts. He knew they required freedom to learn. But he also ensured they felt the accountability.

When one young engineer had lost a critical client meeting because he was out late the previous night, Prithvi did not rebuke him in public. He spoke to him in private, outlined the effect, and reminded him kindly, "Freedom is sweet, but responsibility is sweeter. If you want to continue enjoying night parties in the future, you need to keep happy the one who pays for it: your clients." The young man lived by those words for years.

To the older employees, he offered respect and reassurance. He requested them to lead the juniors, respected their experience, and never discarded their prudence. When one older employee fought against a new process, labelling it as "fashionable gibberish," Prithvi did not counter. He requested him to attempt it in parallel with the previous mode and decide for himself.

A month later, the man conceded that the new procedure saved time. You were correct," he admitted, "but thank you for not pushing." In that equilibrium, freedom for the young, deference to the old, he achieved harmony.

It was not a conflict-free culture, but a rich learning culture. Younger staff members started to value the discipline of the seniors, and the latter learned to appreciate the juniors' creativity. It was like brothers and sisters of different ages under the same roof, quarrelling, competing, but ended up being tied together by love.

Those who repeatedly failed to keep their ego out of the gate soon found themselves where the ego was to be kept.

What emerged from these practices was not a workplace of fear but of belonging. People began to tell stories, passing them down like folklore. Stories of salary structures that forced savings, of sisters lifted into independence, of bonuses tied to holidays, of open cash boxes rarely abused, of mistakes handled as lessons rather than punishments. They became part of the company's culture, told to recruits as if they were parables. And slowly, the organisation came to feel less like a corporate machine and more like a community.

It was in these years that Prithvi's philosophy of compassion began to take its truest form, not as a slogan but as a lived practice. He knew that compassion had to be consistent, not convenient, not only when it was easy or visible. Just as a parent's love is unbroken, his compassion for his employees could not be selective. And in turn, it transformed them, from sceptics into believers, from colleagues into kin, from a workplace into a family.

In the first months of his leadership, as the new culture was just beginning to take shape, Prithvi decided to hold an all-employee meeting. It was not to announce a new policy or to lay out targets, but to talk to them as a father might talk to his children about life. They gathered in the conference hall, many expecting some long speech about productivity or profitability. Instead, he began with a question that caught them off guard.

"When you were children," he asked, "what did you dream of buying when you started earning?"

The room went quiet. People glanced at each other, unsure if it was a serious question. Then, slowly, hands went up. Some said books, others said toys their mothers had refused to buy, dolls, cars, even aeroplanes. He nodded at each answer, smiling. Then he asked again.

"And when you were in college? What did you dream of buying with your first salary?"

This time, the answers shifted. A pair of Nike shoes. A new phone to replace an old one. A solo trip. A fancy watch. Dreams had grown with age.

"And what," he asked softly, "did you actually buy with your first salary?"

The answers turned tender. A silk saree for a mother. A new smartphone for a father. A pair of shoes for siblings. The room grew still as people remembered the look on their loved ones' faces when they received those gifts.

"Why?" Prithvi pressed. "Why did your dreams change? Why did you not buy the Nike shoes or the solo trip?"

The answer came in murmurs. "Because we felt like giving it to them… they sacrificed for us… It made us happy to see them happy."

He leaned forward. "Exactly. You gave because you loved them. You gave because somewhere inside, you knew that your real happiness lies in giving to those you love. You gave without expectation. You didn't ask what return you would get. You didn't measure it. Their smile, their tears, were your return."

He paused, letting the silence hold. "That is who you are from six o'clock in the evening until the next morning at eight o'clock. You live to give without expecting. Then you come to work, and suddenly everything changes. You think only of what you will get, how much increment, how many holidays, will I get a free T-shirt, a bottle, a bag, a bonus? Why does your mind change here? Why do you become someone else?"

The hall was silent. They shifted in their seats, uneasy but thoughtful.

"I want you to be the same person," he said gently. "One person, twenty-four hours. Not two. Don't split yourself between home and work.

Bring the same love and responsibility here. Give without expectation, and you will find you receive more than you imagined.

I will make sure you and your families are safe, cared for, and guided. Just as I do for my daughters. But I cannot do it if you are two different people. Be whole. Be one."

For many, it was the first time they had heard a leader speak this way. Some brushed it off as idealism. Others felt something stir inside them, a memory of why they had once wanted to work in the first place, not for perks, not for status, but for meaning.

Not everyone found this comfortable, though. One bright HR executive, after five months in the company, walked into his office with a resignation letter.

Prithvi asked, "Did we make you feel at home during your stay here?"

"Very much, Sir. You have always treated me as your kid", answered the HR executive.

Prithvi then signed his resignation letter.

The young man lingered, surprised. "Sir, don't you want to ask why I am leaving?"

"No," Prithvi replied.

"Was I not doing well?"

"You were doing great."

"Then why don't you want to know?"

He looked at him calmly. "When a child abruptly decides to leave the home, without ever speaking of trouble, what is the point of asking why? If you had spoken earlier, maybe we could have worked on it. But if you choose to go without a word, what is left to discuss? I don't waste time on sudden resignations of those who were treated as family."

The young man grew defensive. "I felt like I had no freedom. You interfere in everything. It felt like a… a Lala company."

Prithvi chuckled. "Do you know what Lala means? It is what people in the north call proprietors who get involved in every single decision of their small firm or shop. Do you know why they do it?"

"Because they don't trust their people", said the HR executive.

"Maybe, maybe not. But tell me, don't you think parents keep a close eye on their children in the early years? They monitor everything. Why? Because they are instilling values. Later, when the child has grown, they step back. If you have children one day, and they call you a Lala for watching them too closely, will you stop? Or will you say you are shaping them? I am building something that has never been built here in India. I need to be involved in everything, just as a parent is, until the culture grows strong. One day, you will understand."

The resignation stood, but the lesson lingered.

Even the outside world tested his philosophy.

Early in the life of the plant, a labour inspector came for an audit. He asked to see the attendance register. Prithvi told him there was none. The inspector was shocked. "How do you track in-time and out-time?"

"We don't."

"Then how do you know if people are working their hours?"

He smiled. "We don't measure hours. We measure ownership. Do you keep a register at home for when your children enter and leave? Do you time their meals, their play, their sleep? No. You trust them. If you trust them, they become trustworthy. Why should it be different here?"

The inspector left, shaking his head, half disbelieving, half admiring. Although he did insist on maintaining an overtime register as part of labour law compliance. Prithvi implemented that; however, his approach was different still. He asked the employees to enter their overtime hours in the register on their own. No monitoring mechanism, just a culture of trust and self-approval. Prithvi also asked HR to pay them their arrears.

Word of the exchange spread through the factory like wildfire. Employees told each other with pride. It became another story, another piece of folklore that defined who they were.

Through each of these examples, his central point became clearer: rules and policies could force people to perform, but only trust could make them willing to perform. Compassion was not a management tool for him; it was the core of life, applied to work.

Trust, for Prithvi, was never something he wanted hidden in lofty words. It had to be lived out in small, tangible gestures that everyone could see and feel.

Stories piled up, each one a thread in the fabric of trust.

The notion that employees were children was more than rhetoric. He meant it in every aspect.

Children required guidance, sometimes tough, sometimes soft. They required freedom, but they also required correction when they went astray.

He applied the same balance to his leadership.

When a person was irresponsible, he corrected him.

When a person was struggling, he raised him.

When a person was flourishing, he supported him without envy.

It was an approach to parenting, translated into management.

To the outside world, it was not practical. Some suppliers laughed at him, and some competitors called him foolish. But the people who worked with him started to notice outcomes that could not be accounted for by using spreadsheets.

Employees lasted longer, worked harder, and invested more of themselves because they felt like they belonged, not because they were worried about losing their jobs.

Families prayed for him in secret, watching their spouses and children come home less heavy.

Suppliers also began to notice. For he had not limited himself to employees. But his philosophy had instead stretched to suppliers too, the philosophy that said: "Treat your clients and suppliers like your spouse, and your employees like your children."

He practised this philosophy in real terms.

Once, a supplier's shipment of casting and forging materials to Prithvi's company was delayed due to a labour union strike. Instead of threatening the supplier, Prithvi offered to visit their facility to see if he could help. The next morning, he spent a full day observing the plant and then told the supplier, "You've done everything to provoke a strike."

The proprietor, surprised, asked what he meant. Prithvi explained, "I saw workers being frisked at the exit and monitored constantly. How can you expect workers treated with such mistrust to stay committed and to generate cash for you every day? These practices drove them to unionize."

Over the next week, the proprietor implemented some simple changes. A couple of years later, he called Prithvi to say, "Sir, the labour union has been dissolved by the workers themselves. Like yours, we now operate without one. Thank you for treating us as a partner and helping us improve."

In another instance, a global food giant was setting up a greenfield project in India, a major opportunity for both Prithvi's company and its competitors. Known for premium quality, Prithvi's products were priced 30% higher than the nearest rival.

He candidly explained that, being a new set-up, most of the cost came from manufacturing overheads and depreciation expenses, and that, despite the higher price, profits would be slim. The client appreciated the honesty and placed the order.

A few months later, Prithvi's finance manager emailed the client with the subject: "Purchase Order Value Amendment Request." The email explained that savings on unabsorbed overheads had resulted in higher profit margins than expected and hence had requested a reduction in the contract value.

The client's purchase manager immediately called Prithvi: "In 25 years, I've seen suppliers asking to raise prices due to steel costs or inflation. I've never seen one ask to lower a contract. You guys truly live by your values."

With such steps, over the course of time, Prithvi developed a network of clients and suppliers who believed in him, who were willing to go out on a limb for him because they knew that he would do the same for them.

It was folly to some. It was marriage to him, sharing with your partner in times of plenty and times of need.

For Prithvi, it was just living what he practised: that kindness is not frailty but courage, and that relationships are not exchanges but unions.

Suppliers whispered about him in admiration, saying, "This man negotiates as if we are his family."

And clients, although they negotiated aggressively, frequently said that he was one of the rare ones who followed through on his word, even when it was difficult.

To him, these were not tactics. They were not even decisions.

They were the way he knew how to be.

Just as a father cannot cease being a father at the office, just as a husband cannot cease being a husband when he departs the house, so too he could not divide mercy from leadership. It was all the same life, lived with one heart.

This completeness was what distinguished his leadership.

In a world where businesses attempted to tie people down with contracts, he tied them down with trust.

Where others asked for receipts, he provided open boxes.

Where others kept track by hours, he accounted by ownership.

Where others treated suppliers as vendors, he treated them as spouses.

And where others treated workers as resources, he loved them as children.

It was radical, yes, but it worked. Not because it was efficient in the short term, but because it was human in the long term.

People longed for places where they were trusted, where they were loved, where they were treated as more than cogs in a machine. He gave them that, and in return, they gave him loyalty, creativity, and commitment that no contract could buy.

Prithvi firmly felt that home and work were not two worlds, as everyone else attempted to make themselves believe. He felt them to be strands of the same cloth.

"You cannot be an honest man at home and a dishonest man at work," he would remind them.

"You cannot be a fair & caring father at home and a biased boss in the office. You are one person, twenty-four hours a day."

If you fragment yourself, you will shatter. His own life had been the proof. And the same discipline he enforced in the workplace, he brought home.

This belief prompted him to try things that other executives would have been dismissive of as sentimental.

Over the years, Bloam International had started to capture market share from a seemingly monopolistic market. Rivals also found it tough to recruit talent from them.

Clients, suppliers, partners, and employees had started to become one single cohesive family.

From this milieu developed even more stories, each of which contributed to the folklore that defined the company.

Even the ones who departed from the company, mainly for a 30% wage hike as per the unwritten industry norm for changing jobs, took these lessons along. Years on, when they reminisced about their career, they would state, "I learned compassion in that place. I learned to trust them. I learned that mistakes are not the end." Some emulated those lessons wherever they went, taking along a culture sown by one man's belief.

Many who had left Bloam International felt out of place in the new company when they were either micromanaged or had policies that indicated mistrust.

When some of them expressed a desire to return to Bloam International, Prithvi would respond, "We can always create positions for culturally aligned performers, with one condition: you must rejoin at the salary you left at, adjusted only for the inflationary increment you would have received had you stayed."

With annual inflationary increases ranging between 5–8%, this often meant rejoining at a salary lower than what they were currently earning elsewhere. But Prithvi was firm; he would not be unfair to those who had remained loyal to the company.

Despite this, many chose to return, valuing the respect, trust, and mental peace that Bloam International consistently provided. They would say, "It's a unique place which is high on work pressure, yet zero on stress."

The most lasting effect, though, was within the company. Compassion had, over the decades, not been a management tool but a culture. It had converted sceptics to believers, staff to family, and a workplace into a household. Policies went in and out of fashion, markets went up and down, yet the stories remained, binding the company together like glue that was invisible but indomitable.

For Prithvi, there was something obvious about this approach.

It produced human beings, not merely employees.

It brought out loyalty, not because individuals feared being punished, but because they loved.

It made providers partners in truth and not enemies in negotiation.

It built a kind of resilience that no policy manual could match.

He had demonstrated that leadership did not involve commanding people but bringing them up, taking care of them, moulding them, just as a parent would to a child. He had demonstrated that clients and suppliers were not ledger lines but relationships to be loved like a partner. And he had demonstrated that if compassion is at the centre, all else, trust, loyalty, productivity, even profit, follows naturally.

His philosophy never made it to textbooks or chiselled onto banners. It existed in human beings, the way they treated one another, the way they spoke of their years under him. It existed in the tales that were handed down to the generations to come, tales that continue to resound whenever somebody says, "This is how it was when Prithvi led us."

And maybe that was the biggest success of all.

Not that he created a business, but that he created a culture.

Not that he commanded with power, but that he commanded with kindness.

Not that he ordered with laws, but that he ordered with love.

Because ultimately, his life itself was the testament to his own words: compassion is the strongest command.

Story 2: Leadership – The Work Behind the Word

There is a sort of hidden change that occurs to an individual over time, the one that gradually forms the manner in which you think, react, and command. When Prithvi reflected upon his own life, that was what hit him most. It was not one defining turning point, nor a drama-filled success tale that had shaped him; it was an endless series of average days spent discovering what leadership actually involved, days when he messed up, questioned his decisions, doubted his abilities, and yet still refused to abandon the quest to be better.

The young man who had entered the working world with passion and drive had, through the years, become the individual whom people sought advice from. But that transformation was not natural; it was with knocks, learnings, and an almost neurotic desire to comprehend people, rather than merely control them.

Initially, just like most early-twenties professionals, he believed leadership meant being the cleverest in the room, the one with answers, authority, and presence. But life has its way of shattering illusions.

His initial years in the working world were humbling and eye-opening. He worked in small operations where the distinctions between disorder and order were narrow. There were decent folk trapped in poor systems, bright minds choked by narrow hierarchies, and managers who demanded results without knowing how they were accomplished. These were not healthy environments, but they were schools of a sort, each of them instructing him in how not to be a leader.

The years since were full of movement, new work, new teams, and new duties. He worked his way through assignments that pushed him to his limits, sometimes beyond. But behind every test was an underlying need to learn, not only about the business, but about people.

He had come to realise that organisations in their essence were not about numbers, but about cohesiveness. The process may have appeared to be efficient on paper, but if the people working on it were uninspired or fearful, then it really did not matter.

One of his first lessons on self-confidence and being goal-centric arose from frustration.

Early in his career, at 23, Prithvi was sent as site-in-charge to a remote greenfield beverage project in Maharashtra. The role was meant for an experienced manager, but when the incumbent abruptly left, Prithvi, though inexperienced and still serving his induction training, was deputed to fill the gap.

The team included an electrician named Ahmed, about whom everyone had warned him: "He's ill-tempered, inattentive, and always earned a C grade in appraisals. Just avoid him." Ahmed lived up to that reputation, abrasive, hostile, and visibly rebellious, but his expertise was undeniable. He knew his craft better than most managers and carried the gravitas of experience.

Their first meeting was tense. Ahmed openly questioned taking instructions from someone younger than his own son. Prithvi, without arrogance, asked pointed, practical questions about deadlines. Ahmed tried to resist: arriving late to work, often even skipping site visits, showing no interest.

Months passed. One morning, Prithvi confronted him: "The site finishes in three months. Civil works and equipment are ready. Your electrical work hasn't started. What's your plan?"

Ahmed claimed he could complete it in two weeks. Prithvi sternly warned him, "Fail, and the security guard will show you the gate. I mean it." Ahmed, taken aback, confirmed he could meet the deadline.

During a casual conversation, Prithvi noticed Ahmed hadn't been home for 11 months. He offered, "Go home for a month. I'll manage your attendance." Ahmed moved, left quietly. Thirty days later, he returned a changed man. The site was completed successfully, and for the first time in 35 years of work, Ahmed earned an A in his appraisal.

Years later, having changed jobs and lost touch with his former colleagues, Prithvi unexpectedly ran into Ahmed on a train. The man, now sporting a long beard, hugged him tightly, tears streaming down his face.

"Sir, how could Ahmed ever forget the one who gave him his first A grade?" he said.

Ahmed went on to explain how that recognition had transformed his attitude toward his colleagues and his work. Struggling to control his emotions, he then asked, "Sir, tell me honestly, would you really have fired me, knowing well that you couldn't have completed the site without me?"

Prithvi smiled and replied, "I meant it. It wasn't about you; it was about the project deadline. I would have found another technician locally."

Both men, seemingly tough on the outside, wiped away their tears and hugged once again.

As he returned to his seat, Kiran asked who Ahmed was. Prithvi replied, "If Ahmed hadn't happened to me, I wouldn't have learned leadership traits so early:

Treat people as humans.

Let titles be responsibilities-not ego massager.

Stay focused on the goal despite challenges.

Be fearless in doing the right thing. And

Always believe in yourself.

Years later, another lesson on fearlessness came when Prithvi joined a multinational as a Business Unit Manager. The unit comprised 70 people from 12 previously independent sub-companies, each with its own culture. Overlaps in client visits and fragmented practices caused inefficiency.

Prithvi proposed multi-skilling and forming dedicated Learning & Development teams, one for each subject-matter expert. Among them was Mahesh, an exceptionally talented but arrogant manager, whose exclusivity with a major client made him untouchable. The Managing Director even advised Prithvi to tolerate Mahesh's attitude.

As consolidation began, Mahesh tried to mobilize resistance. One morning, Prithvi went to his office to understand why he saw no value in the plan.

The response was explosive. "You can't put experience on paper," Mahesh snapped. "You'll never get it."

But Prithvi didn't complain. He just said, "Perhaps. But if you're the only one who knows, the company is always in your mercy. Don't you want people to remember you for what you've created?"

Mahesh retorted, "I don't get paid to create more Mahesh here. I can't diminish my value in the company to save some cash for the company through your multi-skilling consolidation effort. The company has been running this way in the past, so let it run the same way."

Prithvi remained composed and said, "Fair enough. Do you think I am doing the wrong thing?"

"What you are doing is a good thing and should have been done years ago. But I can't put my job at risk for the sake of the right thing," answered Mahesh.

"You know it well that the other eleven are afraid of you and hence are not getting aligned. You have earned your father figure status with years of learning and hard work. By creating more Mahesh, you shall be signing yourself up for bigger roles by de-risking your current position. So, your employment shall be safer by getting aligned than by not."

By now, Mahesh got agitated. His tone became more abrasive, especially after hearing a threatening hint that his job is at stake if he doesn't get aligned. In a threatening tone, he said, "You are new to the company, so you don't know who I am. Go ahead and try to fire me. The management will not allow you to and might ask you instead to quit, as they know they can find another Prithvi but not another Mahesh."

Prithvi picked up Mahesh's desk phone and called up Vice President-HR, asking her to prepare Mahesh's termination letter while he went and spoke with the Managing Director.

Prithvi got up from the seat while a stunned Mahesh was still looking at him, trying to figure out what he had just heard.

Prithvi went straight to the Director's office and said, "I have bad news for you. While coming to work today, Mahesh was hit by a bus and passed away. Shall we discuss how we will continue to run the company without him?"

The managing director seemed in deep pain. Before he could say anything, Prithvi said, "Easy. That's not true. But can we discuss if it ever gets true?"

Prithvi narrated the whole story and how such toxic people who fail to get aligned should be weeded out for the larger interest of the organisation. They also discussed how to handle Mahesh's clients and to get another manager's retina scan registered with that client.

The managing director supported the decision, and Mahesh was out of the company within the next few hours.

Suddenly, the other eleven became aligned and more productive. A year later, the consolidation project became a success, saving more cash for the company. People became more productive. Higher revenues. Better profits. More important was that while other business units remained fragmented, Prithvi's SBU became known as a single cohesive unit. Moreover, this project was so successful that later the same concept was adopted globally by the company.

To him, retaining a toxic person was riskier than losing a good one. He could be patient with bad performers; he always believed in first aligning people to the culture, but what he could not put up with was the toxicity of the people who weren't ready to get aligned. The message it conveyed, to the rest of the organisation, was that nobody was too big for culture.

On Prithvi's last day at work in the company, Mahesh had come to see him, tears in his eyes, and said, "I was wrong. You did the right thing. I deserved to be fired. I am still jobless. Can you help me find a job?"

Prithvi spoke with HR and recommended that they hire Mahesh not as an employee but as a third-party agent to work on sales commission.

That day reinforced what Prithvi had gradually come to realise:

Leadership isn't about making people happy; it's about creating a conducive space where they can grow.

In time, that faith became his guiding force.

He learned to be at peace with being misunderstood. Leadership, he discovered, sometimes involved being the bad guy in another person's story for a time. It involved doing what was right, not what was popular.

He began developing a leadership style that was not corporate in nature. He was hard but just, blunt but smooth-sided, exacting but gentle. He insisted on responsibility, as he also granted trust freely. He did not believe in micromanaging, although he never cut himself off from the details either.

His principle was simple: when people are trusted, they do their best. He also believed that this trust must be combined with confidence, which must be highly transparent. He always saw trust and confidence as two different things, but very connected to each other. Trust without confidence means nothing, and vice versa.

There is something about working with individuals that cannot be studied from books. No degree will show you how to win people's trust. No business school will instruct you on what to say when a grown man has a meltdown in your office because he's too scared to lose his job.

He had worked both sides of the spectrum, the leaders who held their teams in power by fear and the leaders who inspired loyalty by respect. Throughout the years, he opted for the latter, not because it was less demanding, but because it lasted longer.

There were moments when his patience was pushed to the limit. Leadership, he learned, was not just a matter of making grand decisions at the meetings; it was of the subtle, unseen moments when character was put on the line.

One such incident occurred when the company was negotiating with a client who had promised a huge order but insisted on a "special adjustment", a codename both parties understood to imply unethical compromise. The team was split. The head of sales was saying it would be foolhardy to turn it down. "It's not personal," the man explained. "It's business."

But Prithvi would have none of that thinking. Business was personal for him. Each transaction embodied the soul of the company. The deal was abandoned. The client moved to a rival.

For weeks, some within the team would mutter that he was being idealistic. But the company didn't fold. Actually, the message it conveyed to employees was stronger than the contract they'd lost; it conveyed that they worked in an environment where ethics were not negotiable. That was more important than any spreadsheet could ever be.

It was about being able to look into the mirror and not blink.

His office was not a fortress, and he never had any use for distance between him and his people. No grand gestures, no flowery speeches; there were simply infinite little encounters that defined the place's spirit. He addressed people as a friend would. He asked about birthdays, remembered employees' family members' first names, took a keen interest in their children's aspirations, mentored many such kids so they achieve their aspirations, called up families, and stood by them rock solid in times of need. It wasn't about being a nice guy; it was about being there.

He had witnessed business firms where the leaders understood everything about market trends but nothing about those who made their products happen. That imbalance unsettled him greatly. He opined that a leader who doesn't know the faces behind the figures will have to face the music someday.

The business experienced a reflection of his personality. With colleagues and time, it was no longer just a place to work and was beginning to resemble a space shared in purpose. Lunchtime laughter, the soft hum of respect in hallways, and an unwritten code that individuals were more important than titles existed.

He used to say, "If you switch to a different computer screen when your manager passes by your desk, it means I have failed somewhere in building a culture of mutual trust." He would encourage people to feel free to do their personal work during business hours because the reverse was true, too.

One day, while walking to a meeting on the first floor of the facility, Prithvi noticed a machine operator on the ground floor intently looking at his cell phone, standing next to a CNC machine. He told his team to start the meeting without him because he had a more important task to accomplish first, and went down to the shopfloor. The operator quickly hid his phone in his pocket.

Prithvi put a hand on the operator's shoulder and asked, "May I know why you stopped watching when I came?"

"Sorry, Sir," the operator muttered.

"It's not about sorry. I genuinely want to understand," Prithvi replied.

"Because you pay me to build products, not to watch videos on a phone," said the operator.

"That's not true," Prithvi said. "If you do your job well and on time, feel free to watch videos, check WhatsApp messages, or chat with friends and family, just never at the risk of your safety. Safety comes first."

Seeing the operator relax, Prithvi teased, "Can we watch the video together now?"

The operator blushed. "No, Sir. It's an adult-only type."

Understanding, Prithvi advised, "Never do anything that could embarrass you or your family if it were publicized tomorrow." The operator nodded, embarrassed, "I promise, Sir."

Prithvi added, "To make this real, the first thing you do at home today is share your phone passcode with your high school daughter, Vijayalakshmi."

Weeks later, Prithvi found himself sitting next to the operator in the canteen during lunch. Smiling, the operator said, "Mission accomplished, Sir. When I shared my phone passcode, Vijaya immediately shared hers. My wife and I always worried about the kind of friends she would make at such an adolescent age. Now all three of us know each other's passwords, and there's mutual trust in the family. Thank you."

Prithvi smiled, "That's great. But don't check her phone. Never do policing on those who trust you. The fact that she shared her passcode shows she's aligned with your family culture. Trust her blindly, and she would never prove you blind."

His disciplinarian style was just as different. He was not fond of public scolding. When you would do something wrong, he would call you in, sit you facing him, and have a low-key conversation with you.

"What did you think went wrong?" he would say, "Tell me."

The larger majority of the people sank off before he could say a word. It had not been guilt, but realisation. He made them look at the mirror.

He felt that shame wasn't a penalty; it was a reflection that made individuals better.

He would say, "Do wear multiple hats but not multiple masks."

That wasn't to say he was easy. In fact, he was disarmingly tough when the occasion arose. Folks learned his kindness was always within boundaries. If someone betrayed trust, second chances didn't exist. But if someone erred from a place of honesty, he stood up for them with ferocity.

A middle-level manager once botched a client relationship that resulted in a monetary loss. The man entered Prithvi's office, his face flush with anxiety, bracing himself for a reprimand. Instead, however, he was confronted with a query. "Did you hide it?"

The manager confessed that he had immediately told his seniors about it.

"Then," said Prithvi, "you've already done the hard part. Mistakes, I can forgive. Lying, I can't."

There were other times as well, times that showed the more nuanced sides of his style.

These included a rare talent for being able to see potential in people that others did not. He felt that everyone should have an opportunity to show their stuff, particularly those who had been given up on only because they were introverted or reticent.

His technique for finding talent was unconventional. He would give tough assignments to those who were labelled average, quietly, to find out how they coped under pressure.

It wasn't a test of ability; it was a test of character. There was also a technician called Bala who toiled unobtrusively, never spoke up in meetings, and was generally overlooked by his seniors. Prithvi observed that Bala never left until the job was complete.

One day, without warning, Prithvi assigned him the task of running an entire client site single-handed for a month. The order elicited suspicion.

"He's not leadership material," someone murmured.

Prithvi did not react. One month on, the client wrote a handwritten note complimenting Bala on his professionalism. The same individuals who had doubted him now viewed him in a different light.

That was how Prithvi wanted his lessons to go, not by lecturing, but by outcomes.

Leadership was, however, not only about developing others, but also about confrontation. He feared not calling out misbehaviour, even if it was from individuals whom he respected.

One day, a seasoned sales performer who had gotten a huge contract single-handedly was caught cutting corners to close deals quickly. His rationale was the classic one: "The end justifies the means."

Prithvi did not agree. "It never does."

The man was asked to leave. The financial loss hurt for a long time because of the magnitude of sales he used to bring, but the moral clarity it restored was priceless.

That philosophy informed all of his choices. He wouldn't create a successful company only on paper. He wanted it to be something that could make people proud.

There were moments when his compassion manifested in unexpected ways. He understood the smallest things that impacted morale, the manner in which a superior addressed a driver, the tone of an email, and how the housekeeping staff was treated.

It was a way of life for his teams. Folks began to treat each colleague with respect, whether they were executives or custodians. It wasn't mandated; it was felt.

Yet, even as he cared deeply for his people, he never lost sight of accountability. He believed that care without accountability breeds entitlement. And entitlement, to him, was poison. He had seen it destroy many good companies. So, he put across the point that compassion did not imply complacency. The individuals were at liberty to commit mistakes, but not at liberty to remain irresponsible.

All through, his office was the heartbeat of the company. People went in scared and came out enlightened. They knew that in case he was angry, there must be a cause. He never shouted, but when he did, he loaded it with truth. His anger was never personal but instead founded on principles. That made it all the more potent.

The team members came to realise what leadership was by just observing him. They noticed the way he treated every issue as his own.

If a worker's equipment broke down, he didn't summon a meeting; he went to the shopfloor himself.

If there was a complaint from a client, he would personally go to the site and listen.

Not because he did not trust his managers, but simply because he felt that leaders should never become too settled behind their desks.

He always believed that parents always work harder, and so should leaders. His belief in the fact that leaders at work should work harder than their team was firm.

Gradually, people started owning problems instead of passing them around. People stopped saying, "It's not my job." They started asking, "How can I help?" And once that shift happens, an organisation becomes unstoppable and sustainable for generations to come.

Prithvi had witnessed it.

He had witnessed the haggard look of technicians transform into bright smiles.

He had witnessed juniors initiate without being asked to.

He had witnessed individuals putting in extra hours not because they had to, but because they wished to.

The HR Manager once recalled asking Prithvi about proposals to extend work hours from eight to twelve, a direction many companies were beginning to consider.

"We've seen you consistently encourage people to go home on time and spend time with their families, so I wanted to know your thoughts," she said.

Prithvi smiled and replied, "Do you know why I get upset when I see people working beyond business hours or on weekends, often ensuring I don't get to know of this?"

"Because you care for us," she said.

"Partly correct," he said. "But there are other reasons too. One is Parkinson's Law, which states that work expands to fill the time available. If we extend working hours to twelve, people may end up producing the same output they currently deliver in eight, unless we first address the root causes." He continued, "Those root causes are usually inefficiencies which can be addressed by going deeper in analysing who is doing, why he is doing, how he is doing, and what tools we have provided to them. Extra hours are a signal that something is flawed. We must identify and fix those inefficiencies before asking for more time.

"Another reason is work overload. Even when we have the right people doing the right thing, working the right way with efficient tools, extended hours may still occur simply because we've loaded them with too much work. That, too, needs to be identified and corrected."

He paused before adding, "Even machines, whose only job is to work, have endurance limits. We humans carry many responsibilities beyond our jobs, and such oscillation between responsibilities is the beauty of human life.

Our people often work extra hours anyway, for two reasons. First, because of the sense of belonging that comes from the vision-led work culture we have built. Second, because we never demand extra hours. The more tightly you hold a child within boundaries, the more they try to resist and break free. Try at home by asking your child that she has no other option but to study for twelve hours every day, and watch her productivity versus appreciating her for studying so hard, and asking her to take a break between long study hours. You will find her productivity shoot up.

The day the order incoming rate becomes faster than the shipment rate, we will first investigate all the above, before gathering again to find the next course of action."

That was leadership, not policies, not goals, not motivational speeches, but a silent passing on of intent from one heart to another.

And best of all, maybe, was that none of it took place overnight. It developed gradually, as trust always does.

Each day brought its new question, its new challenge, and its new profundity of knowledge regarding what it really meant to be a leader. This was mixed with periods of success that made him take pride in, and times of exhaustion that made him question whether it was all worth it.

However, in the middle of all this, there was always something that remained constant: he never lost his values.

Expansion was accompanied by complexity. The teams grew bigger, the stakes increased, and the choices became more complicated. What had been a straightforward responsibility, leading a handful of people, was now controlling thousands. Each choice reverberated across departments. Each error could cost not only dollars, but trust. But Prithvi had reconciled to this weight. He considered that if you want to lead, you need to know that isolation is part of the job.

He had seen what leaders do when they are under the strain of popularity. To him, leadership was not about popularity. Instead, it was like parenting, doing the right thing for the family, consistently, regardless of gaining momentary respect.

There was a time when that consistency was severely tested. The company had ventured into a partnership that was intended to catapult them to a new level of growth. It was a high-risk deal that needed a huge initial investment. The entire leadership team was pumped, with one exception: Prithvi. He felt a whiff of something unnatural. He found everything great about the company's product except for the owners. He found a culture mismatch. He did not find them transparent. He brought up his issues in a meeting but was defeated.

The Finance Head stated, “If we don’t seize this, someone else will.”

The marketing director came in with, "We cannot allow things to fizzle.”

But Prithvi didn't believe it. He did not dislike ambition; he just did not like to jump into things. The argument became heated. Some of them accused him of being too conservative and theoretical. But he did not yield.

"Let us do what is right for the company, not what is thrilling for the moment," he maintained.

A few weeks later, client documents showed secret clauses that would have caused the company to face harsh penalties. His intuition was not wrong. Nor did he brag of being right. He merely remarked, “This is the reason we never play games with trust.”

It was among the silent victories, the ones that are never written but save entire organisations.

Every decision drained him. But every decision strengthened him, too.

There was one incident that would haunt him for years to come. Two of his top employees, both geniuses in their own right, had fallen out harshly.

Their animosity had started infecting the culture around them. Office corridors hummed with gossip. Teams had started taking sides. It was no longer about a professional difference of opinion; it had turned personal.

The HR chief attempted to mediate, but nothing seemed to work. The tension was spreading like a slow burn.

Prithvi summoned both of them to his office. He did not yell, did not take sides. He merely invited them to sit and speak. For more than two hours, he heard each one of them pour out their anger. When they finished, he said something neither of them anticipated.

"You both are right," he stated calmly. "And that is the issue."

You two are trying to win when the business requires that you work together. He stopped and let his words absorb.

"The day your ego gets larger than your purpose, you cease being an asset. And you both know that in the balance sheet, what is not an asset gets recognised as a liability. And I don't carry liabilities. Choice is yours!"

There was a silence in the room. The two men did not meet each other's eyes. Eventually, one of them collapsed. The other did too. It was not the end of their differences, but the start of understanding. Slowly but steadily, things had started to change from there between them. Years later, they would look back on the meeting and say it was the day they really learned about leadership.

Prithvi could see through people. He didn't merely read what they said; he read what they did not. He picked up on body language, tone, silences, the subtle cues that betrayed truth. He could detect when a person was speaking out of conviction and when they were standing behind excuses. This acuity wasn't manipulation; it was empathy honed into insight.

His talent for reading emotion grew into one of his strongest attributes. He would often advise that a great leader is someone who learns to see the individual behind the employee.

That sensitivity had not weakened him; it had strengthened him. When individuals felt heard, they worked differently. They ceased working in fear and began working in faith. And faith, he considered, was the greatest motivator of all.

But empathy did not imply indulgence. He did not confuse understanding with accepting subpar behaviour. He was ready to assist anyone who was in need, but not anyone who was irresponsible.

That was the thing about him, people knew he wouldn't tolerate dishonesty. When someone had commented that there's always a degree of honesty, so we need to weigh it before taking any tough call, he would term honesty as digital, either yes or no. They could argue with him, disagree with him, or even challenge him. But they could never deceive him. And that made people act differently around him. His presence itself became a moral check.

He frequently framed leadership as parenting, not paternalistically, but in the context of needing patience, discipline, love, and consequence.

"A parent doesn't scold or counsel a kid because they like it," he once explained. "They do it because they care enough to correct."

He applied the same thinking to his employees. His job was not to shield them from discomfort, but to ready them for reality.

He spent an enormous time mentoring young managers. He'd tell them that leadership wasn't about authority, it was about accountability.

"Don't expect respect just because of your title," he would say. "Earn it by being the first to take responsibility and the last to take credit."

Those who understood this grew into remarkable leaders themselves. Those who didn't eventually faded away.

And maybe his biggest achievement was not that he created a solid company, but that he created solid people.

Even in times of crisis, when money was short or spirits were low, his level-headedness was infectious. There were moments when others panicked, and he wouldn't.

He brought that conviction to every situation. A fiery client meeting or a tough termination, he did it all with a quiet dignity that settled everyone around him.

He also did not think leadership was supposed to be glamorous. It wasn't sitting up in a cabin and issuing decrees.

It was being present when things were difficult. He used to walk through the factory floor late at night, visiting night-shift workers, talking to security personnel, observing the minute details, the hum of machines, the pace of work, and the spirits of the people.

They kept him earthy. They reminded him of why he did what he did.

He never enjoyed being addressed like a "sir." He insisted that people use his name. Feel free to call me by the name you call me behind my back."

The result: some called him Big B, some Gurudev, some called him by his first name, and some called him Sadhguru.

In all his years, he had watched those companies with brilliant logos and glossy pamphlets topple under ego.

He'd also watched those lower-key, humble operations flourish just because their guys were interested in getting things done correctly.

It was that belief that formed the second act of his leadership.

He started to change his emphasis from operations to culture, for he knew that great companies are not built by systems, but by values shared.

The first thing he did was take down the silent walls that divided people. Titles were reduced, hierarchies dismantled, and chat was fostered. He didn't want fear present. Fear, he used to say, kills curiosity. And a workplace devoid of curiosity becomes stale.

He wanted people to question, to argue, to bring better ideas to the table, even if those ideas went against his own. It was not a statement to be said with wisdom; it was a challenge. He did not desire blind followers. He desired thinkers.

During one meeting, a young graduate trainee hesitantly disagreed with his strategy for a client presentation. The room fell silent. Prithvi could see everyone looking at him as they expected an answer.

Instead of pulling his brows, he leaned back and smiled. "Convince me," he said.

The young man was shocked and justified his reasoning one step after another.

At the conclusion of it, Prithvi nodded and told him, "You are right. Let's do it your way. And you are going to lead this client presentation."

The culture was transformed by that little incident. Individuals studied that bravery was not a punishment, but rather a reward. They also learnt that with bravery came accountability, as Prithvi had asked the trainee to lead the presentation so that the trainee gets the learning that it's not only about providing *'a preach'* or an unsolicited *'gyaan'* but also about demonstrating it. And the young man who was initially hesitant went ahead to lead a big project several years in the future.

Prithvi used to say that being a leader does not mean that we are always right; it means making an environment where the right ideas will arise. He never feared to be corrected. What irked him more was silence, for silence represented fear.

He also felt that individuals had to be trusted before they could learn to be dependable. So, he started constructing systems that substituted faith in place of control.

Spending approvals were streamlined. Decision authority was decentralised. Individuals were given the freedom to make their own decisions within parameters.

"Let them feel ownership," he stated. "The ones who abuse it will quit, and the ones who warrant it will thrive."

His philosophy succeeded better than anyone had hoped.

Departments that once depended on constant monitoring began working with stealthy effectiveness.

Managers began mentoring rather than policing.

The company evolved from a chain of command into a network of collaboration.

When an individual had a case to be appreciated, he ensured that he did so. In case somebody was supposed to be corrected, he ensured it was done in a dignified way.

He created a tradition that made its way to the genes of the business in the form of handwritten thank-you letters.

When a person had ever done anything extraordinary, either a big job or a simple act of kindness, he would sit and compose a personal note and would place it on his or her desk. It was not a piece of art; it was as simple as one sentence sometimes. But people treasured those notes. When he came to visit somebody a few years later, he could see one on the wall.

That was his method of granting effort quietly, not with fanfare. He felt that praise in public could humiliate people who were humble by nature, but a note of thanks behind closed doors can remain in their hearts for a lifetime.

Once, the Chief of Sales suggested introducing awards like "Star Salesperson of the Year" and "Best Sales Region of the Year" at the annual sales conference, believing it would encourage healthy competition. Prithvi immediately rejected the idea.

He explained, *'It's either healthy or competition. At home, do you compare your children, saying one is better than the other? No, you know it will spark a cold rivalry and reduce care and support between them. It is such small acts that lead to the 'crab mentality'.*

We shouldn't do anything that divides our work-family either. That's why we won't call it a sales conference or limit participation to sales alone. Let's make it an Annual Gathering, including everyone across departments."

Such moments were becoming legends that employees shared with newbies. Legends of how the Managing Director would go to the kitchen to personally thank the cook for a perfectly prepared lunch. How he once spent an hour assisting the maintenance team in repairing a faulty air conditioner. How he would not accept moving to a more luxurious cabin even when his bosses offered him one, since he did not believe in physical distance from his colleagues.

Those stories weren't included in a company guidebook; they were included in a living memory that influenced the way all of them conducted themselves.

He had a strange method of determining the type of person who was suited for leadership.

Rather than using reports of performance, he paid attention to how people acted when no one was observing. Did they give credit? Did they offer to assist others? Did they remain calm under pressure?

These, in his mind, were indications of leadership.

Prithvi generally called his management style tough love. He was hard, yes, but he never anticipated people doing something that he did not want to do. He became a part of the team when there was a deadline that needed to be met. In cases where there was an issue, he addressed it directly instead of shifting the blame. People had a belief in him, not because he was a perfect person, but because he was a real person.

The genuineness of his existence created a loyal following that could not be purchased with money. Workers remained for decades, sometimes rejecting higher offers, because they felt a sense of belonging that could not be replicated with cash.

"It's not a job anymore," one of them once said. "We are a family now."

Prithvi knew that well. For him, leadership was always relationship first, responsibility second, and title last.

He was aware that when you're leading, people don't necessarily hear what you have to say; they sense what you sense. So he protected his energy jealously. He ensured that even on bad days, no one in his presence felt left behind.

There are some moments in every leader's life when the world appears to challenge the level of conviction that lies in them. For Prithvi, those moments arrived when the business faced turbulence.

It was not one devastating blow, but a gradual constricting of events, increased costs, slow payments, uncertainty in the market, and, most of all, exhaustion in the system.

People were weary, exhausted, and anxious. They turned to him to show them the way.

He had always believed that the real idea of leadership was not in success but in struggle. Anybody can be smiling as things work out. Still, to remain calm when the whole world around is disintegrating requires more than bravery. That takes faith.

At that time, each morning was a new crisis. Some were technical, some financial, and some just emotional. There were projects that derailed, clients that defaulted, and employees who became restless with uncertainty around ongoing geopolitical situations.

Prithvi saw the fear spread like smoke through the corridors. He knew he couldn't deny it was there. But he couldn't allow fear to win either.

He did not keep things from his team either. He never sugar-coated. He spoke to his people the truth, the failed targets, the slow payments, the coming obstacles, but in the same light, in the same breath, always in balance with faith. "We've come this far because we did things the right way," he would say. "Let's not change our way just because life got harder."

He didn't hold a town hall or fire off a corporate email. Not his style.

Instead, he started walking more through the office, speaking with people in informal groups, eating with them at lunch, joking with them, and listening more than he talked. His calm didn't diminish the challenge, but it provided others with something even better, reassurance.

He felt that hope isn't delivered by words; it's delivered by energy.

One afternoon, when a particularly important client cancelled a long-term service contract without warning, the service head stormed into his cabin, agitated. "We've lost everything," he exclaimed. "This will ruin the quarter."

Prithvi didn't respond immediately. He looked out the window for a moment, then turned and said quietly, "We've lost money, not everything."

"We'll earn it back," Prithvi added. "But let's not lose our people's confidence in the process."

And he meant it.

In the days that followed, instead of cutting costs blindly or downsizing departments, he focused on communication. He saw opportunity in such times of adversity.

He explained the situation transparently and reassured everyone that no layoffs were coming. "We're going to ride this out together," he said.

Prithvi asked every employee to submit a plan for a single assignment: 'This is how I will generate more cash for the company.'

He held small meetings, guiding HR and Finance team members who thought cash generation was only the sales team's job. He explained that saving cash is as valuable as earning it.

By the deadline, the company buzzed with ideas. HR proposed multi-skilling and enhanced learning & development to boost productivity. Finance suggested minimizing invoice errors and speeding up accounts receivable. Engineering streamlined part number creation and improved first-time-right efficiency. The shop floor team came up with Value Stream Mapping ideas for making processes leaner and improving workflow.

The company adopted a festival-like energy to implement the ideas. Employees could spend money if needed without seeking approval, and all suggestions had tight deadlines. Lean business days became opportunities to improve efficiency, while the front-end team pursued new revenue. Productivity dipped briefly, but morale stayed high, and no one quit.

In a world where many leaders disappear behind excuses during bad times, Prithvi's visibility became his strength. His team began to trust him more, not less, during the crisis.

To him, leadership was never about faking it. It was about being brave enough to stay authentic.

And authenticity, he discovered, made something special happen: resilience.

The firm gradually began to thrive. Newer products were launched, aligning with the new global market trend towards lowering dependency on fossil fuels. The company became much efficient and lean in processes. Profit margins improved. The clients who had previously withdrawn started coming back as the market revived. People heard that this was a company that wouldn't sacrifice its values. And that, more than any advertisement, became its brand.

But even as the business stabilised, there arose new problems, this time from within.

Expansion had attracted fresh faces who didn't yet feel the same passion for the firm's culture. Prithvi sensed the change, little telltale signs of ego, territoriality, and complacency. It bothered him greatly.

He resumed old traditions, the personal memos, the impromptu lunches, the open-door meetings.

He went to internal reviews unexpectedly, not to spy, but to listen. If he caught someone cutting off a junior during a meeting, he interceded softly. "Allow them to finish," he'd tell them. "We all learn more by hearing."

It was his means of reminding everybody that humility was not up for debate.

His leadership philosophy had developed by then. No longer did he think a leader was there to fight fires; he was there to prevent sparks. And prevention, he discovered, came by way of culture.

He created programs that fostered teamwork.

One of them was beautifully straightforward.

Departments were required to nominate each quarter a person from a different department who had contributed to their success. It compelled individuals to recognise interdependence, to understand that no one succeeds alone. The exercise started as a ritual but gradually became a source of happiness. Individuals began paying attention to the kindness they would have otherwise overlooked.

One day, a group of veteran managers approached Prithvi, venting their frustration. "This new batch never comes on time for meetings; five minutes late seems normal," one said. Another added, "They're always glued to their phones, disturbing everyone with alerts, or even taking client calls mid-meeting to look busy."

The HR Manager shrugged, "We've tried to mould them, but you know how millennials are."

Prithvi smiled. "Funny, isn't it? The same millennials you complain about are eagerly waiting at home for you every evening.

Be assured, starting tomorrow, you won't see them late to meetings. Go back to your work."

He then asked the Admin Manager to buy fishbowl glass jars, two for each meeting room, and digital clocks. By afternoon, everything was set up. Prithvi dictated a note to accompany them:

- Anyone arriving even a minute late must drop the smallest currency note in their wallet into the first jar. No coins. The digital clock's time is final.
- The same penalty applies if a phone or computer makes noise during the meeting.
- The second jar is for the meeting organizer: if the meeting exceeds its scheduled time, they deposit the smallest currency note multiplied by the number of attendees.

The admin manager printed the instructions and placed them with the jars.

Within a week, the jars were full of cash, yet another open cash pool in the company with no surveillance. Some even kept only a five-rupee note handy to avoid penalties.

What started as a playful experiment quickly became a game-changer. Meetings started on time, punctuality became a habit, and the impact even got extended to improvement in client deliveries. Even fearless millennials enforced the rule while visiting clients, who, amused, happily contributed to the fishbowls. Discipline had become fun and contagious.

That, Prithvi believed, was the manner in which culture was constructed, through teaching individuals to perceive goodness.

But he was also practical. He didn't have any belief in utopian visions. He understood that every team would contain tough personalities, individuals who lived for conflict or fought change. But rather than doing away with them at once, he attempted to discover what their inspiration was. He found out that most tough guys were not bad guys, just misunderstood, insecure, or afraid. His sense of being able to go beyond behaviour and into emotion put him ahead.

One time, one of his most talented and most unstable employees made a scene at a client meeting by arguing with a senior publicly.

The HR team wanted to send him a warning letter. Prithvi told them, "Let me speak with him first."

He took the employee into his room and asked him to sit. "Do you know why this irks me?" he asked. "Not because you took exception, you were entitled to because I see that as courage. But because you showed disrespect to somebody in public, which I see as a violation of core values."

The eyes of the young man welled up. "I didn't say it like that," he whispered.

"I know," said Prithvi. "That's why I'm speaking to you and not sacking you."

That discussion had its lasting impact on the employee.

Prithvi possessed the ability to make even those disciplinary situations learning opportunities. He did not want fear to be the motive that made people comply. He did want understanding to be the motive that made them learn and change.

There was another incident that revealed how profoundly his sense of fairness existed. One of the clients presented the firm with a profitable assignment on the provision that one of their more experienced engineers, a person who had questioned them regarding quality issues, be substituted.

It was a simple business decision to take, but Prithvi declined. "If a man's integrity bothers a customer," he explained, "that's a client we don't need."

The room became quiet. The opportunity was gone. But something even more precious was acquired, the unshakeable respect of each individual who worked for him.

That one act soon became legend within the company. It reminded everyone what type of organisation they worked with, wherein their Leader chose an employee over a big client because the employee was right. He also felt that leadership involved showing the guts to criticise even the top performers when they crossed the line.

There was a time when a top salesperson, renowned for his numbers, started treating backend staff poorly. When the issue reached Prithvi, he did not call for a formal inquiry. Instead, he strolled to his desk and quietly said, "Your results impress me. But your behaviour disappoints me. Fix it before it gets immaterial to fix."

The man was shocked.

He did fix it and never forgot that moment.

Prithvi understood something few leaders do, that greatness isn't measured by how high people rise, but by how gracefully they rise.

His attention to small details extended far beyond performance reviews. He noticed the tone of internal memos, the wording of client replies, and even how office chairs were arranged during meetings.

To some, this level of involvement seemed excessive. They called him a "Lala" leader, someone who meddled in everything. But he didn't mind the label.

"If caring about my people makes me a Lala," he said once, "then I'll wear that badge proudly."

He used to always say that the soul of an organisation resides in its minute details.

As time passed, folks caught on to the fact that his type of leadership was not about being a company man. It was about developing a generation of individuals who would take his principles into their own workplaces. His impact filtered quietly, through routines, through examples, through tales spoken in awed whispers.

He was no longer merely a manager or a founding MD. He was a philosopher.

Time alters all things, the structures, the visages, the cadences of a workplace, but for Prithvi, most of all, time altered his connection with leadership. What was once the pursuit of excellence gradually turned into a practice of grace. He no longer assessed success by growth or gain; his gaze rested on quieter, more subtle triumphs, the kind that fail to reach annual reports but remain in the lives of individuals.

By that point, he had lived many iterations of himself already.

The young upwardly mobile professional is struggling to prove himself.

The mid-level restless leader is learning how to balance compassion with command.

And lastly, the veteran Managing Director, whose very presence could calm a room.

But through all of those iterations was one consistency: he never ceased being a student.

Early on, he led through effort. Midway, he led through systems. But in these latter years, he led through wisdom. He no longer had to be everywhere and control everything. His presence was less about telling and more about inspiring. People no longer obeyed his command; they emulated his example.

He had created an organisation that reflected his inner values, demanding but warm, disciplined but profoundly humane. You could feel his spirit in the way the people smiled to greet one another, in the tone of the discussions which filled the corridors, and in the assurance with which even the most diminutive employees expressed their opinions.

And still, he never permitted that success to lull him into complacency. In fact, it made him more watchful, more considered. He understood by experience that the instant a leader believes that his culture is invulnerable, erosion starts quietly.

He still paced the floors, although the company had expanded well past those initial rooms. He still stopped to acknowledge the housekeeping staff, still listened for someone's tone on the phone, being impatient, still picked up between the lines in reports others read in haste. In his mind, leadership was not about size, but detail.

On one of the days, he visited an office of one of his clients with his management staff and noticed that the nameplate on the wall with the name of the firm was slightly crooked. He stopped, set it right himself, and grinned.

His employees laughed, yet the point was made. In that one easy gesture was contained a whole philosophy: notice things people take for granted.

That was the way he upheld his legacy, not through great speeches or legislation, but by steady example.

His door was always open. Employees across the board understood they could enter to discuss an idea, a concern, or a blunder. And, as they entered, they were not met with criticism but curiosity.

He recalled how difficult it had been for him, as a young professional, to go to authority figures. Fear of being shot down or mocked kept people quiet. He vowed never to be that type of leader.

At one meeting, he was quiet in the group. His silence was no lack, but a presence. He was also a good listener who gave people a chance to complete what they were saying, even when he did not agree. Words were significant when he spoke since they were limited and considered. When he was speaking, people inclined their heads forward not according to any sense of duty but to show reverence.

With time, he acquired what many referred to in the company as "the Prithvi effect." It was hard to put into words, but everybody sensed it, the soothing confidence that no matter how complex situations became, someone at the helm was thinking rationally and would always make the correct decision.

So, as he would say, “no need to panic unless it’s a matter of brand image or safety, which once lost, rarely gets regained.”

It was not charisma. It was not charm. It was integrity.

He had become the organisation's moral compass. They used his name as a verb: "Do it the Prithvi way," they'd say, when referencing decisions made with conscience.

But with that respect came loneliness. The more esteemed he became, the more isolated it grew. People started seeing him as infallible, someone who had solutions for everything. Not many were aware that behind that calmness, there was a man who carried all the burdens of the people without complaining.

He never viewed his path as an individual triumph. And that self-awareness informed his humility.

He wouldn't take credit for the success of the company publicly. When the press or partners credited him, he would at once deflect the praise to his team.

He wasn't being humble for show. He really believed that without humility, leadership is hollow. Even when he had the right to exert his dominance, he preferred to listen.

He had realised that leadership, at its finest, was not about ordering others about, but about releasing them. It was about noticing what individuals didn't yet see in themselves and having the guts to challenge them to rise to it.

As his years serving as Managing Director went by, he started to spend more time mentoring himself than managing himself. His emphasis shifted from fixing problems to showing others how to fix them. He had a profound sense of fulfilment in seeing the leaders of the next generation take over, individuals who had been raised under his tutelage, now leading others with the same philosophy. He was most proud when they disagreed with him thoughtfully. "That's when I know I've done my job," he once said. "When they stop looking for my approval and start thinking on their own."

He believed that the real measure of a leader's legacy is how many people continue doing the right thing when you're not around to remind them.

By then, the systems and culture of the company had taken on a life of its own. He did not have to impose values anymore; they self-organised. They were punctual, projects were progressing without any hitch, and people were respecting one another, not because they were compelled to do so, but because it was in their collective DNA.

But to step back wasn't easy. For a man who'd lived every stroke of his professional life through purpose, releasing the daily rhythm of leadership felt like trying to unlearn breathing itself.

He dialled it back slowly. He began to pass more things along, to completely trust the next generation, to let them learn from their own mistakes. He knew that true leaders do not create followers, but more leaders.

He didn't cling to power; he passed it over with grace.

It had shown him tolerance, tolerance that lets you sit quietly when every bit inside you is yelling at you to do something.

It had taught him restraint, the power to maintain a cool head at a time when everything around you is going haywire.

And above all, it had taught him to be humble, to realise that no matter how elevated you are, you remain a human being, you are still subject to error, and you must continue to learn every day.

There was a certain serenity in his later years that people often spoke about. It wasn't the serenity of retirement or detachment. It was the calm of someone who had made peace with his choices, the kind of peace that comes when you've given your all and no longer need validation.

That philosophy had carried him through decades of governance. It was what kept him level-headed even when it got tough. He had been betrayed, criticised, and lost some loved ones. He had lost loved ones he never imagined he would. He had witnessed ideas falling apart that he firmly believed in his heart. Yet he never allowed bitterness to creep into his heart.

He never viewed leadership as a crown that would be given, but a mirror that had to be cleaned day by day. Your values, your choices, your tone, your truth reflected in a mirror.

He never used to make a splash on goodbyes, and when he at last came to the point of making his last goodbye, he was not in the mood to make it either. But his people wouldn't allow it.

They planned a quiet evening, not a flashy corporate sendoff, but an evening of warmth and remembrance. The auditorium was packed. Technicians, directors, customers, suppliers, ex-employees, even the ones he had once fired, they were all there. There were words of speeches, there was laughter, and even some tears.

When a customer stepped onto the stage to speak appreciatively about Prithvi and Bloam International, Prithvi rose from the back of the auditorium and walked down the aisle toward the stage, gently interrupting him. Taking the microphone, he said:

"May I ask you all not to record anything that is said here today? Over the years, we have built an iconic family, one in which employees, clients, and suppliers are all part of a single family. What will be spoken tonight comes straight from the heart. I would hate for any of this to end up on social media or be used as customer-speak or a marketing tool. Let this evening remain just that, an evening for all of us."

The crowd erupted in cheers.

Even on his last day at work, he had passed on a powerful lesson to his people.

And when his turn arrived to speak, he stood for a moment or two in silence before he spoke, "My purpose in life is to touch lives and to establish the fact that a long-lasting business empire can be built on moral values. Nothing beyond."

People walked differently for days after that evening. There was this increased awareness, this subdued pride of being a part of a space that was characterised by a man who had been a leader so clear, so understanding.

His teachings were still remembered years after his retirement. Staff would recall his advice when making tough decisions. His words echoed in meeting rooms, advising people through problems no longer relevant for him to solve. His reputation had turned into an unobtrusive, moral presence, felt but invisible.

And perhaps that was the strongest demonstration of leadership. Not power. Not authority. But influence that lasts longer than your title.

Even years later, when new employees would ask seasoned employees what had changed about the company, they were told the same thing: "It's not what we make here that matters. It's how we make it. It's the way we treat each other. That's what he taught us."

Prithvi had created the nest of eternity in the world where speed, strength, and success had become the standards most of the time, a civilisation based on the principles of decency, discipline, and dignity. It was having an understanding of oneself to the extent that one could lead others without losing his/her balance.

And that made him unique.

Story 3: The Client is the Business

Looking back on all the years that have gone by, what Prithvi can remember is not the size of the transactions that he made or the complexity of the projects that he handled. Rather, it is the innumerable moments of awareness between people; those small decisions that strengthened relationships in a way no strategy memo could achieve.

For Prithvi, the client was never a number on a report or a logo on a slide. The client was a living, breathing human being, one who believed in him with their work, their stress, their name, and sometimes even their late-night worries. None of that trust could be quantified through revenue charts. It had to be earned, one conversation at a time, one problem solved, one expectation exceeded.

He never did believe in selling. That term bothered him, like it was insisting on persuading someone to accept something they didn't absolutely need. To him, it was always a matter of understanding, viewing things the way the client was viewing them, sensing the sense of urgency of their dilemmas, and talking their language without assuming to be superior to them.

Well before the market started talking about client-centricity as a business philosophy, it was just the way he did things. He wasn't working from a formula; he was reacting instinctively, with integrity, with a sense of proprietorship that made each client's challenge intimate.

That frame of mind came early, before there were structures or systems. Back then, he'd frequently go alone to see a client, sitting across from them at their office or factory, listening attentively to what concerned them most. He would see small things, the tone a manager used when discussing downtime, or the look of frustration in an engineer's eye when a product did not work as claimed. Rather than pitch with features and specs, he'd say, "What keeps you up at night?" That single question opened more doors than any pitch could. It caught people off guard, and most of the time, they told him the truth.

That truth was the foundation of all the relationships he established. He learned early that the majority of clients did not require another vendor. They needed a partner, someone who genuinely cared enough to be responsible. There were instances when it would have been convenient to cite the details of a warranty or to shelter under a policy.

But Prithvi never had faith in taking cover behind forms. If there was a problem, it was his to fix, and not theirs to control.

There was one such tale that his teams still narrate, a big order that had been done and delivered within time, a milestone celebrated. After months, the client complained of a tank leakage problem. Most would have sent a welding support team, marked the complaint closed, and forgotten.

But Prithvi didn't even think of that as an option. He called up his engineers, informed them they would redo the whole defective system at the company's cost, and personally guaranteed the client they would never have another problem. It wasn't an easy call. It had cost money, time, and human power that the company could hardly spare during those times. But he never calculated the price for doing the right thing.

He calculated the cost of what would happen if the client lost faith in them. That choice was a tale that spread far beyond the bounds of that particular project. In their internal meetings, the client would often recount the incident, how the leakage had ultimately been traced back to their own water quality, and yet Bloam International had quietly replaced the entire system without a word of complaint, the industry took note, and the team learned something that would stay with them for years: that doing right for the client was not an expense; it was an investment in credibility.

It was in moments like these that Prithvi's conviction deepened.

There was one other night that was still fresh in everyone's minds. It was the eve of a client's grand opening ceremony of their green field project, wherein all the equipment was supplied by Prithvi's company. Equipment installed, banners printed, guests invited, all set.

But in the final test, one of the engineers realised that a set of components had a machining concentricity problem. The product would still perform with such an issue for a couple of years before failing. The convenient option was to overlook it, allow the inauguration to go ahead, and surreptitiously replace the parts later. But that wasn't how things were done when Prithvi was in charge.

In minutes, he had made up his mind to redo the whole batch. By midnight, the team was back at the factory, labouring under white lights, sleeves rolled up, refusing to stop until every piece had been reworked. At 2:30 a.m., a vehicle finally pulled out of the gates, beginning the 600-kilometer journey to the client's site, carrying the reworked parts along with the welders and fitters who would see the job through. By 10:00 am, the inauguration proceeded smoothly as silk. No one in attendance had any idea about the backstage drama, but the client did.

That one act of integrity, solving an issue before it occurred, embodied what partnership was all about. He never preached team ethics or delivered sermons on values. He just behaved the way he believed business should be conducted. He taught through actions.

It wasn't a question of how much the client would purchase; it was a question of how much they would trust. And gradually, that trust became their greatest differentiator. Business rivals arrived and departed, many offering lower prices and more brassy promotions. But those clients remained. Some had been there for decades, going from one firm to another, taking the relationship with them.

"We do business on value and values, not on price," Prithvi used to say. It was an easy philosophy, but it took guts. There were times when margins were tight, and a lower price point could have filled the order book with ease. But he wouldn't budge.

"If we play the price game," he advised his leadership team, "we cease to be us." His philosophy wasn't based on emotion; it was based on hard-won experience. He had witnessed what occurred when companies pursued quick profits, how they torched relationships, how clients learned to anticipate less and question more.

Partnership for him was not a phrase for handouts. It was the daily habit of honouring what you say, even when it hurts. There were a few times when that habit was put to the test.

Once, a client in the northern part of India entrusted Prithvi's company with the complete plant design and supply of products for their massive project. The scope also included supervision of project execution, so Prithvi's team had deputed one of their Project Managers on-site full-time. Any delay in project completion would cease the tax relaxation offered by the local government.

The project had progressed smoothly and reached the commissioning stage when, one late evening at 10:00 PM, the General Manager texted Prithvi to report an accident at the site. The GM planned to rush there on the first flight the next morning. Prithvi called her and asked her not to travel, as she was due to deliver a baby in few months, and instead requested the Project Manager's phone number to take charge personally.

On the phone, the Project Manager was crying and even offered to resign immediately. After speaking with him, Prithvi realized that the accident had occurred due to the client's fault: one night-shift operator had accidentally charged a pipeline, causing a collapse and burst. Rather than owning up to the mistake, perhaps because of its magnitude, the client had shifted the blame to his Project Manager, which had resulted in him getting nervous and emotional breakdown.

Recognizing the gravity of the situation, not only the accident but also the potential delay and penalties to the client, Prithvi decided to visit the site himself rather than delegating it to someone else. He took an early morning flight to Delhi and reached the remote site by road that evening.

It took twenty-one days to redo the entire setup and commission the plant, well ahead of the deadline. During this period, Prithvi ran his company, Bloam International, remotely, operating from a single table and chair in a corner of the site.

This gesture embarrassed the client as well; they saw how challenging it was for him to manage daily site progress while simultaneously running his company. One evening, the night-shift operator met Prithvi in private and confessed to the mistake, a confession the operator's own company had never received. Prithvi honoured that trust, ensuring the operator's name never surfaced.

Time has passed since that incident, but it has become timeless, shared multiple times within Bloam International and by the client. It remains a rare example of an MD running his company from a client site for twenty-one days, just to ensure the client was in safe hands.

That reputation quickly started to spread faster than their advertisements. New clients would find them, not due to advertising, but because someone else had said, "They'll stand by you." When trust was a commodity that didn't come around often in this business, that made them who they were. It wasn't rosy, but it was strong. Even when the bigger competitors attempted to undersell them, the clients knew lower didn't equal safe.

They knew Prithvi's people or Prithvi himself would show up when things went wrong, and that was worth more than any discount.

Inside the organisation, this culture created its own rhythm. Targets were important, but they were never allowed to overshadow the real purpose. Rather than pushy selling, they engaged in courteous listening. Rather than pursuing numbers, they pursued problems to be solved.

That took more time initially, but it established relationships that lasted years, and those relationships, in turn, established stability.

So he protected it vigilantly. When clients complained, he required that they answer with humility, not defensiveness.

"If they're complaining," he would say, "it means they still value us. The day they stop complaining is the day they have moved to others."

Most of his principles were a reflection of a very human approach to business. He had the conviction that each client, irrespective of size or scale, should be treated with dignity.

There was a case of a small firm whose proprietor had purchased only a couple of units. One of them kept failing. The effort to service that client far outweighed the value of the order. But Prithvi never gave up on him. "It doesn't matter how small the order," he said. "It matters that he trusted us."

Because only one of the two units, installed on identical process applications, was failing repeatedly (about once every 15 days), identifying the root cause proved extremely difficult. The team replaced components again and again, 31 times in total, before the issue was finally resolved. The breakthrough came only when the company's Design Manager and QA Manager stayed on-site for 15 days to closely observe the unit's performance.

The order resulted in a significant financial loss for Bloam International. However, the long-term payoff came years later, when the same client became a loyal advocate, generating multiple referrals.

It wasn't a marketing strategy; it was the natural outcome of decency. Through all of this, Prithvi's leadership remained understated. He never made grand declarations about client focus. Rather, he infused it into the company's everyday conversation.

He encouraged his managers to walk the floors of the client's building, to observe how their product was being used in real life, and pick up thoughts for newer innovations.

Several of the firm's most successful products didn't originate in boardrooms but rather on clients' sites. Whenever they ran into repeated problems, Prithvi urged the engineers not to be satisfied with temporary solutions. "Let's own the issue," he would instruct them.

This ideology created a culture of ownership that obliterated the distinction between development and service. Each complaint was an opportunity, each frustration a hint. The engineers started viewing themselves not as manufacturers but as problem solvers, individuals who constructed solutions that simplified clients' lives. Even in the toughest markets, this approach set them apart.

Rivals tried to copy designs, undercut prices, and make promises they couldn't keep. Prithvi paid them no attention.

"We don't get paid by our rivals," he told his sales team. "We get paid by our clients. So, let's focus on creating real value for them, stay true to our purpose, and let competitors do whatever they choose."

He knew that if they stayed true to their values, the clients would see through the noise.

And they did. While others worked on closing, his people worked on opening. The payoff was slower, but it was long-term. He also used to think empathy was not a weakness; it was a strength.

There was one account of a young sales engineer who spent months going to see a potential client without success. Every meeting ended in the same manner: polite discussions and no commitment. But he persisted, not to sell but to comprehend.

One day, incidentally, he gave his seat to an elderly lady on the bus, not aware that she was connected to the same client he had been making calls on. The act reached the client, and the next visit was different. The sale went through, not due to tactics, but due to empathy.

Prithvi used to tell that tale, not to draw attention to luck, but to illustrate that the person you are beyond the work is just as important as what you do within it. To him, all client interaction was a reflection of the company's values. It wasn't sufficient to do what was done; they needed to do it the way that was done, with dignity, with patience, and with consistency.

He frequently referred to the idea of being "embarrassment-proof." As he contemplated any action, he would ask, "Would we be comfortable if this ended up in tomorrow's newspaper?" It was his mechanism for ensuring every decision would withstand the test of integrity.

That question became an unwritten rule throughout the organisation. They utilised it in conferences, in negotiations, and even in vendor meetings. It became a part of their ethical DNA.

His partnership mentality went beyond the business fences. There were times when clients encountered crises that were unrelated to his products, financial challenges, plant shutdowns, and supply chain problems. In those times, Prithvi didn't stay away. He extended assistance, occasionally logistical, occasionally just ethical support. “We’re in this together,” he would say. Those gestures were never forgotten. Years later, when markets shifted and contracts came up for renewal, those same clients would say, "We remember who stood by us."

It was through such experiences that his philosophy evolved, that the client is the business. Not in the sense of dependency, but in recognition that everything meaningful the organisation achieved flowed from the relationships it nurtured.

If the client prospered, they prospered. If the client struggled, they had to come in and assist in stabilising the ground. It was not charity, but it was a partnership in its purest sense.

He had his life founded on that principle. For him, success wasn't about growing faster or getting louder. Instead, it was about remaining loyal to the people who put their trust in him, particularly in the times when it mattered the most.

Moments like these defined him. To the people who worked with him, Prithvi's calm decisions in moments of pressure became quiet lessons in leadership. He never raised his voice, never made dramatic declarations. He just did what was right, again and again, until it became muscle memory for the organisation.

His office was never a closed door. Clients often walked in without a scheduled appointment, frequently with issues, and sometimes just confused, and he just listened, as if he had no other task. Listening, actual listening, is a lost art in business, and yet, Prithvi honoured it. He was incredibly good at listening without interruption and allowing people to finish a thought, even if he already knew what they meant. That was disarming patience. The majority of clients were not accustomed to being heard. They were accustomed to being managed.

With Prithvi, they discovered someone who would listen before he would reply. That was the basis of his client philosophy, experiencing the world their way. He would frequently explain to his managers that recognising a client's issue didn't imply blindly agreeing with them. It suggested that he could put himself in their shoes. He would say, "If you can see their problem through their lens, speak with them in their industrial process language, then you have addressed half of it."

He never worked in transactions; he worked with humans. He did not distinguish between empathy and efficiency. The two were one with him. He would visit a client's factory or location, not necessarily because there was a pending issue, but simply to witness. He would work alongside their engineers, questioning them about things that weren't business-related: What was the most difficult thing they did each day? What frustrated them? What would make their life simpler? He wasn't at the location to sell something. He was there to learn how they operated. Those visits created bridges that no marketing budget could. Clients came to regard him as one of their own, a person committed to their advancement, not merely his.

This intense sense of ownership sometimes embarrassed his staff. "Sir, this wasn't our mistake," they would complain when something failed because of a client's internal error. But Prithvi would shake his head. "They trusted us," he'd say. "If they're having an issue and we can resolve it, it becomes our issue too."

It was that desire to own something that many times resulted in some of their biggest breakthroughs.

One day, an old client from the chemicals business had a continual problem with one of their filtration systems. It wasn't their product that was malfunctioning; it was one of their external components provided by another supplier. The convenient solution was to inform the client to repair it themselves. But Prithvi identified a business opportunity within the hassle. "If they are experiencing it, others will have too," he explained. He recalled his engineers, brainstormed night after night, and created a product that included the absent filtration feature. The outcome was not only a satisfied client but also a new product line, which turned out to be one of their top-performing categories.

Issues, to him, were cues. Every grievance was a map. He would say to his staff, "The client informs you what to produce next. You just have to listen." It was not romantic idealism. It was rigorous curiosity.

Of course, not every client made life easy. There were rough ones, the ruthless bargain hunters, who quoted prices, who pushed limits. But even there, Prithvi never lost his patience. He never believed in matching desperation for desperation.

When one day a client bluntly informed him that a rival had quoted a similar product at a much lower price, Prithvi merely replied, "If you buy today on price, you will leave us someday on price. For if price is the only divergence you can see, we haven't yet demonstrated what partnership is."

There was no annoyance in his voice, only calm conviction. The phrase wasn't practised, but it caught precisely the effect it was meant to. A year later, the same client was back again. The cheaper system had collapsed, and they now appreciated the worth of the difference they had neglected.

They never requested a comparison again after that day.

He had a knack for redefining professionalism. To him, professionalism was less about wearing a tie or firing off well-crafted emails. It was about being consistent, showing up, keeping your word, and doing it quietly.

His calmness in the face of noise baffled many, but his results silenced them. Clients remained because they felt secure. And security, in commerce, is more valuable than any advertising catchphrase.

He was also well aware that compassion had to be paired with toughness. "Partnership is not saying yes to everything," he instructed his managers. "It is showing enough concern to say no when you need to."

There were times clients requested impossible timelines or specifications that sacrificed quality. Prithvi would politely tell them why it could not be done that way. "If I agree today," he would say, "you'll have an issue tomorrow. And that issue will belong to us to resolve."

Most clients appreciated that honesty, even if it was uncomfortable for them. Amidst all of that, one strand remained consistent: his conviction that business relationships were constructed on common purpose. He would always remind his staff that they were not simply producers of a product; they were partners in their clients' success stories. He needed each client to believe that when they allied with Prithvi's business, they were complementing their own organisation with a problem-solving arm.

With the passage of time, this philosophy began showing in what the recruits talked and did. They were taught not to pursue short-term sales but to pursue trust. They were taught that a late order, if presented honestly, generated more goodwill than a flawed delivery accompanied by silence. They were taught that a handshake was as valuable as a contract. And gradually, quietly, the company expanded, not only in size, but also in respect.

Even rivals started recognising it. At a trade convention years later, the Chairman of a competing company, where Prithvi had once worked as a field salesman, walked up to him and said, half in jest,

"I've never faced competition like this before. Your products are strong, but what truly sets you apart is how deeply your people care."

Prithvi smiled and replied, "That's because I learned the hard way the cost of not caring."

They both laughed. The moment stirred an old memory for the Chairman, of a young Prithvi, years earlier, courageously calling out the biases within the organization, only to face character assassination by his manager for refusing to join a favoured inner circle. Instead of addressing those issues, the Chairman had advised Prithvi to accept such biases as a norm of the corporate world.

There was a feeling of subdued pride that went with it. Not arrogance, but confidence, the sort that results from doing things the way they should be done, even when the world doesn't pay you back right away.

For Prithvi, knowing the client wasn't a department's responsibility, it was everyone's. Whether he was an engineer on the factory floor or an accountant preparing a bill, every individual was part of the relationship the firm had established. He wanted everyone to understand the human being making every purchase order. "When you pick up that phone," he would tell them, "Remember, there's a human being on the other side who's got deadlines, pressure, and expectations, just like you. Treat them with the same respect you'd want if the roles were reversed."

That concept gradually began to remake how individuals worked. Shop orders had the client's name mentioned beside the shop order number. Communication grew friendlier, answers became faster, and issues ceased being kicked across from desk to desk. Departments that had traditionally operated in silos began communicating with one another. When a client had a complaint, no one ever said, "That's beyond our scope of contract." Rather, they asked, "Let's try to solve this together."

Prithvi had always felt that a company's character wasn't reflected in its ads or its mission statement; it was reflected in how its people responded to a problem. He used to remind them that they weren't shipping equipment, they were shipping peace of mind. "When a client buys from us," he would explain, "they're buying the assurance that we'll stand by them, not just till installation, but till they no longer need to worry about what they bought." That assurance came with a cost. It demanded vigilance, humility, and relentless follow-through.

But it also created something that money couldn't buy, trust that deepened with every interaction.

The term "client" itself held a certain significance in his organisation. For him, "client" was not a transaction. It implied a relationship. It implied someone who had put trust in you. You don't break it, not even once."

There was a saying that used to ring in the corridors quite often: We don't sell; we serve.

Prithvi was often heard telling his sales team,

"Every number you see on your dashboard represents a client who chose to do business with you. You could never sell even a pin unless the client saw value in what they were paying for." He would then add, "So never carry the swagger of a star salesman, carry instead the pride of someone who knows how to match value to price."

It wasn't a slogan, but a way of life that was lived. Sales calls never started with talk of revenue or targets. They started with talk of what clients were grappling with and how they could be served. When one regional head once proposed more aggressive methods to take market share, Prithvi subtly disagreed. " Trust and respect can't be demanded," he said. "You can only earn it."

He knew that real partnerships could never be founded on persuasion. They had to be founded on purpose. If the client felt misunderstood, no discount or incentive could retain them for long. So he taught his teams to ask better questions, listen longer, and never interrupt when a client was speaking. Sometimes, it involved sitting through long, awkward silences as the client struggled through their ideas.

Those silences, however, usually uncovered what was truly distressing them, the implicit aspect of the issue no one had bothered to ask about. It was in such discussions that Prithvi started realising how many sectors were plagued by the same perpetual gaps, problems that were never addressed because the suppliers were too occupied selling the next item. He wasn't going to be a part of that chain. "If we fix one issue well," he declared, "the next order will follow naturally." And it did.

Gradually, clients began to deal with his business not as a supplier, but as an ally who was able to think with them, rather than for them.

Prithvi's business strategy was never to grow faster; it had always been to go deeper. He liked to say that growth was an outcome, not an objective.

"If we continue doing the things we need to do, growth will find its way to us," he once said to his finance head on a tough year. There was little room in the numbers, and pressure was high, but there was no way he would bend. "We can lose a project," he stated, "but we cannot lose our compass."

Sometimes this positioning puts them at odds with rivals who play by a different set of principles. Rivals who low-bid on prices, who made outlandish promises, and who took shortcuts that clients would only realise months down the line. But Prithvi never wavered from following. He knew that when the dust settled, only those who had done things the right way would still be standing.

When nervous salespeople complained about rivals copying their products and selling at much lower prices, Prithvi would calm them with an example from the banking industry.

"The product there is exactly the same," he would say. "Currency notes. Yet some banks make hefty profits while others collapse."

He reminded them that while products, especially in the era of 3D printing, can be copied, what cannot be replicated is a company's vision and DNA.

"No one ever loses an order on price," he would tell them. "They lose it either on value or on pitching to a wrong target customer."

That belief led him to stop reviewing 'order-lost analysis', which almost always ended with the same reason: 'lost on price.' Instead, he began reviewing 'order-won analysis', challenging the team to replicate those successes with other clients.

Training was redirected toward identifying the right target customer, in increasing value proposition and elevating the client experience, because that, he believed, was the only sustainable competitive advantage.

And time proved him right. The culture he built was not loud or self-congratulatory. It was quiet, deliberate, and deeply humane. When recruits joined, they often came expecting the usual corporate grind: targets, pressure, and competition. What they found instead was something different.

They discovered mentors who valued their integrity higher than their numbers, managers who were proud of honesty even if it meant losing a deal, and an MD who thought that the best way to measure performance was to determine the smile that you left behind. He taught his people to take little, positive things that made clients' lives easier.

If an installation site required additional safety equipment, they shipped it without being asked. If a client's team wasn't able to work a new system, they provided extra training at no extra charge. These weren't big gestures; they were just acts of partnership. They got embedded into the company's DNA over time. Clients picked up on it. They started saying, "With Prithvi's team, you don't have to remind them twice."

One of his lead engineers remembered one time that embodied this spirit perfectly. One of our clients' systems developed a small problem on a Sunday morning. The service team, pre-emptively, took spare parts out without official approval and repaired them by the evening. The next day, after Prithvi found out about it, he raised no issues about cost or overtime.

He just smiled and said, "That's how you earn Sundays that matter. We shouldn't tell customers of getting back the next working day when they were working on a Sunday to share the problem."

It wasn't about the worth of the job. It was regarding the worth of the relationship.

In an industry where surprises were common, Prithvi's company became known for predictability, and predictability became their competitive advantage. The more one watched Prithvi's work style, the more obvious it was that his philosophy wasn't based on management philosophies; it was based on an in-depth understanding of human nature.

He understood that clients and employees remembered how you treated them more than what you provided. So, he made sure that every experience left something behind with a feeling of care and justice.

When a late delivery of shipment was caused by external factors, he penned a personal apology to the client in a handwritten note, duly signed by all employees of the shopfloor. When a client had a daughter who was getting married, he sent flowers and best wishes, again signed by all employees, not because he felt obligated, but because he remembered the client's daughter's name from a casual mention months earlier. Those were not planned things; those were small things that flew out of him. And they personalised the relationships, making them human and lasting.

His client-centricity was not one-dimensional. It was not merely being responsive or courteous. It was about ownership: ownership not just of errors but of aspirations. He had once told his design head, "If our client has a vision, our job is to make it easier for them to get there." It was that looking-ahead empathy that turned his company into a silent partner in the success stories of many clients.

That profound integration created a situation where it was virtually impossible to replace them. Clients came to view them not merely as suppliers, but as being on their own journey, individuals who spoke their language, who empathised with their urgency, who rejoiced in their milestones as if they belonged to themselves.

And gradually, over time, how Prithvi operated started to radiate outward. What had initially been a founding MD's conviction grew to become the company's way of living. It wasn't so much what Prithvi spoke during meetings anymore; it was what individuals did when nobody was looking.

Expansion brought with it complexity, more teams, new geographies, tough clients, and changing expectations. It would have been simple for client obsession to get lost in the din of scale. But Prithvi wouldn't allow that.

He ensured that each new branch, each recruit, and each new manager grasped one simple fact: we are here because our clients trust us, and that trust is never broken.

He started a practice that initially surprised a lot of people. Each year, he would spend some hours going through the annual client feedback survey personally, not only the big ones, but even the minute ones. Complaints, compliments, suggestions, he went through them all. He did not see them as data; he saw them as voices.

To make this annual exercise a real-time event, he introduced a simple idea that worked beautifully: a web link that opened a direct channel to him. Every employee was required to include this link in their email signature.

The message was clear, to clients, suppliers, partners, and employees alike, that anyone could reach Prithvi personally, whether to seek help or escalate an issue.

Many advised him against it, warning that he would be overwhelmed by messages. But his response was simple and unwavering:

"People's safety, and a company's brand image, once lost, are extremely difficult to regain. If being reachable bothers me, then I have no right to be in a role that involves people."

His team knew he wouldn't budge. They were fully aware that Prithvi would reply to every email and text within 24 hours, whether it came from someone inside or outside the company, a senior executive, or a fresh graduate seeking employment. He made himself accessible, always, except for phone calls. The moment someone called without prior notice, he would block the caller. His team knew that if there's anything urgent, they need to call him twice, disconnecting the first call after three rings.

He would explain,

"People who call without checking if the recipient is available are self-centred. I prefer to stay away from such people."

Otherwise, anyone could reach him. He would add,

"If someone reaches out to you, it means they see in you their solution provider, whether for a genuine reason or using you as a ladder step. If I'm too busy to respond, maybe a young Prithvi is getting lost in the cruelty of the corporate world in the absence of a mentor."

It made leadership accessible in a way people weren't used to, and it changed the tone of communication across the company.

What impressed people most about him was how he could then balance compassion with strength. He was not soft; he was direct. When a client once demanded an unrealistic deadline for delivery, Prithvi sat down with their crew and explained to them, openly, what every step entailed and why cutting corners would hurt both of them. "I'd rather you're upset with me now," he told them, "than disappointed later." The client agreed, reluctantly at first, but with gratitude later. And when the project was completed, they thanked him for standing his ground.

That balance, of care and conviction, became a hallmark of how his company operated. It earned them not just clients, but believers. Many clients began inviting his team to their internal strategic discussions, not just as vendors, but as advisors.

They wanted their inputs before finalising new projects. Prithvi took that as the highest form of respect. "When they start asking for our opinion," he said, "we've truly become partners."

He had tremendous respect for long-term thinking. In his view, the real success of a business wasn't defined by profits each quarter, but by the number of clients who remained for decades.

He would frequently say to his leadership team, "The easiest way to grow is to do the right thing long enough."

The market would sometimes turn in mood, sometimes embracing speed, sometimes disruption, sometimes price. But Prithvi remained steady. He would never compromise the company's integrity based on trends. "Fads are meant to fade. Values last," he'd repeat.

When there were new entrants with lower prices, the urge to respond was tremendous. But instead of reducing prices, Prithvi bet bigger on quality. Instead of compromising on cost, he spent on people and process. The outcome was unobtrusive but incontestable, while others ebbed and flowed with market currents, his firm gradually built, layer by layer, client by client.

He believed that excellence was a mark of respect. He would say, "By doing a job well, you respect that person who trusted you." That was a belief that resonated through every function of the firm. From design to delivery. No shortcuts were taken. If a client needed something urgent, the team stayed late. If a mistake happened, it was owned immediately. If someone felt unheard, Prithvi made sure they were called and listened to. Over time, these acts built an ecosystem of reliability. Clients began to associate his company with peace of mind.

Within the organisation, individuals started to imitate his actions. The manner in which they addressed clients altered. The tone became softer, the compassion more profound, the purpose more pointed. The meetings no longer revolved around defending standpoints, but instead around how to solve problems. "It's not us versus them," Prithvi would tell them. "It's us with them." That subtle change turned everything around.

There were occasions, too, when there were errors from clients: mistakes in specifications, payment delays, and last-minute changes in requirements. Rather than responding with anger, Prithvi's team found themselves getting used to responding in sympathetic ways: "If we can get them through their worst days," he said, "they'll reward us on their best." And they did.

What set Prithvi apart wasn't that he never suffered losses, but that he never permitted losses to make him cynical. Even when contracts fell through to lower-cost competitors or wholesale good-faith errors cost them dollars, he maintained faith in goodness. That simple faith kept the company rooted even in rough seas.

As the years passed, many of the early clients became friends. They shared stories, memories, and even personal milestones.

Some of them retired but still kept in touch. They shared that in an ever-growing world, Prithvi's was one of the rare businesses that still believed in giving more than it took.

As his business grew, Prithvi started mentoring young leaders, instilling in them that client-centricity was not a strategy but a disposition. He wanted them to grasp that compassion and capability could happen simultaneously, that you could be empathetic without being weak and ethical without being naive.

He would also tell how, in the early days, he had once decided to lower the cost of an ongoing order because the cost of production had come down unexpectedly. The client hadn't requested it, and they wouldn't have even known. But Prithvi sent an altered invoice. "If we expect trust," he said, "we have to give it first." This single act became company lore. Years later, the same client gave them orders of many times greater value to manage.

He would often think that the world had changed, technology had developed, markets had become uncertain, and clients had turned more demanding, but the principles were the same. "People still buy trust," he would say.

He had always thought that real leadership wasn't control, but conviction. "If I need to remind you of the right thing to do," he said to his leadership team once, "then I've failed to lead." It became a silent mirror that informed their decisions.

By then, the organisation had turned into a living testament of what client-centricity was like when it was practised consistently.

The same ethos that had driven a handful of people in a tiny office now ran through hundreds of people across geographies and functions. From the design engineer to the logistics coordinator, everyone knew their job touched a client's life somewhere, and that realisation altered the way they worked.

Clients who began with modest orders remained for decades. Clients who departed for lower prices routinely came back, thanking him, "We didn't know what we were missing." Those comebacks were never given fanfare or hubris. They were greeted with the same affection as with the initial order, for with Prithvi, each renewed faith was holy.

He used to explain to his managers repeatedly, "As a solution provider, our job is to see beyond what the client can see as their need. And this can happen only when you have spent enough time on their premises learning their systems & processes and mapping those with our offerings."

That was foresight, patience, and above all, care. His teams were taught to see beyond the moment, anticipate a problem before it arose, and consider the next step before the client did. That was the foresight that transformed them from being vendors to partners.

His choices at times seemed idealistic in the short term, but always held up. The trust his company had established became its largest currency. It couldn't be seen on balance sheets, but it opened doors that numbers couldn't. When new clients approached, they came not because of advertisements or pitches, but because someone they trusted had said, "Talk to Prithvi's team, they'll take care of you."

Even competitors, over time, began to acknowledge the quiet power of his approach. Some admitted privately that while they could match prices or replicate products, they couldn't match his consistency. "He's playing a different game," one rival once said. "He's building relationships while we're chasing contracts."

That distinction was precisely what characterised Prithvi. He never let short-term profit determine long-term course. There were transactions he turned down because the conditions didn't match his principles. There were alliances he refused because the other party wasn't on his plane of morality.

He also possessed an uncanny knack for making things simple. When his people were feeling bogged down by targets or pressure, he would remind them, "Just remember why we exist, to solve our clients' problems and to help them live their vision. Everything else is noise." That clarity cut through confusion like light through fog. It reminded people that purpose was their best strategy.

What made his philosophy sustainable was that it wasn't constructed for him. It was constructed for principles that anyone could live by. He didn't want the company to be dependent on his physically being there; rather, he wanted it to be dependent on its own conscience. Therefore, he was pushing people to question any decision that didn't make sense to their own moral code, even if it was his.

If you believe I'm mistaken," he once said to a young manager, "tell me so. I'll not take offence, provided you're looking after the client." That candour was a silent strength. It built an organisation in which ethics were not imposed; they were shared.

After a while, Prithvi's style of work not only affected his company but also his clients as well. Quite a few of them started implementing the same kind of strategies with their clients, motivated by the experience they had witnessed. It was a chain reaction of decency. And though he never took credit for it, Prithvi often smiled when he noticed those echoes in the industry, competitors being more transparent, clients becoming more empathetic.

He was still very humble despite the fact that he had done a lot. He never allowed his success to separate him from others. Thus, when employees visited him, they found him most of the time as usual, approachable, curious, listening rather than talking. "The higher you go, " he used to say, "the quieter and humbler you have to be. Use your ears and mouth in the same proportion."

It was his humility that made him so incredibly genuine and, as a result, people gravitated towards him.

One night, at an internal party, someone asked him what he believed was the key to their ongoing success. He paused and replied, "We never forget that our client is not part of our business. They are our business."

The best indication of this approach occurred many years later when a worldwide slump struck the business. Projects were put back, budgets were slashed, and payments stalled. Many companies struggled to survive. But Prithvi's company stood steady. Their clients stayed loyal. They extended timelines, shared workloads, and even offered early renewals to support the company that had supported them for years. The goodwill that Prithvi had built quietly, one relationship at a time, came back to hold them like an invisible safety net.

When things settled down once again, he brought his leadership group together and spoke quietly, "This is the reason why we do what we do. Profit will come and go, but trust, trust will see us through every storm."

And as they gazed around the table that day, at the faces of individuals who had been on this path with him, they knew he was correct. The numbers in their balance sheet were robust, but what really made them was the unshakeable trust their clients had in them.

In the later years, when one talked about Prithvi, one would talk in anecdotes. They didn't discuss financial success and market rankings; they talked about incidents. About the time, he himself phoned a client to apologise. About the note he wrote by hand when a project was late. About the day that he preferred honesty over convenience, even if nobody would have known anything different.

They spread throughout teams and decades, handed down as legend, plain reminders of how it was to create something of substance. For the newer staff, most of whom had never even seen him in person, Prithvi wasn't some figure in a frame on the wall. He was a presence, an attitude, a subdued standard by which every little choice was made.

He never cared about great legacies. He did not want buildings in his name or awards named in honour of him. "If people recall we made them feel valued," he said one time, "that's all we need." And they did. Clients recalled the calm that resulted from doing business with someone who did what he said he would do. Employees recalled the security of being in a firm where decency was a given. Partners recalled the stability that resulted from his steady sanity.

It eventually became something over time, something more than transactions. It was a philosophy, a belief that it's best to do right by people and that that is the most sustainable business model there could ever possibly be. In meetings, his senior staff would catch themselves parroting his lines, not habit, but by truth. "Let's do what's right, not what's easy." "The client trusted us; that means something." "We'll find the answer together." These words shaped the company's rhythm long after he had stopped saying them.

And perhaps that was his real achievement: he had built a business that no longer needed to be reminded to care.

One afternoon, years afterwards, Prithvi called on one of their longest-standing clients, not for work, just to check in. The client, now grey-haired and soon to retire, smiled warmly on seeing him. "You know," he said, "we've done business with so many firms over the years. But you're the only ones who never treated us as customers. You always treated us as partners." Prithvi smiled. "That's because that's what you are," he said.

Sitting together, reminiscing about those projects that had once kept both of them up nights, the conversation turned to the young generation, to the way they worked differently, quicker, sometimes more aggressively. The client posed the question, "Do you ever fear that the new world won't appreciate this old method of doing business?"

Prithvi paused for a moment before answering. "Perhaps they will phrase it differently," he said. "They will say user experience, design thinking, client obsession. But at its core, it is the same thing, caring. So long as there are those who care, this path will never be out of style."

That discussion lingered in his mind. He understood that what he created wasn't time-bound or trend-conscious. It was anchored in something timeless, the plain reality that people, regardless of how things come and go in this world, will always react to genuineness.

On his final day, he left on his desk a handwritten message to the leadership team. It contained only one line: "If you go that extra mile for those who trusted you, they will never let you fail."

And then for years after that, when the company was ever at a crossroad, a pricing decision, a negotiation, the frame would be gazed upon by someone, and the words would be said, "What would Prithvi have done?" And the response was always pretty much the same: the right thing.

He had demonstrated, through decades of unobtrusive consistency, that if you place people above profit, you don't lose business, you gain it. If you put understanding ahead of persuasion, you don't retard growth, you fortify it. And if you found a company on trust, it doesn't merely endure markets, it outlives them.

Prithvi's journey was not about extraordinary moments, but about extraordinary constancy. About choosing decency, day after day, until it became destiny.

And long after he was retired, that constancy continued to echo in every handshake, every service call, every satisfied smile on a client's face. It was the unseen heartbeat of the organisation, steady, reliable, and unmistakably his.

Story 4: Culture by Design, Not Default

This was many years ago, when Prithvi was in his late 20s, hopping between jobs. It was a bright Tuesday, the kind of day that usually feels full of promise. Prithvi walked through the glass doors of one of India's most celebrated companies, one that proudly called itself "the best place to work." He was thrilled; this was supposed to be a new beginning.

The HR representative greeted him warmly, offered the usual smiles, and said, "Let's introduce you to the team." She led him down a narrow passage toward a cabin where a man sat at the desk Prithvi was meant to occupy.

"Here's the person you'll be replacing," she said casually. The man looked up, puzzled. It was clear from his expression that he had no idea what was happening. When she added, "Prithvi will be taking over from today," the man's face drained of colour.

For a moment, Prithvi froze. He'd assumed the transition was already handled. The HR woman fumbled through polite words about "realignment" and "a new direction," but it was obvious that this was the first time the employee was hearing any of it.

As Prithvi stood there, awkwardly clutching his joining documents, he realised this wasn't a misunderstanding; it was how things were done here. Someone was being replaced without dignity, and everyone around pretended it was normal. The man gathered his belongings in silence while HR busied herself with forms.

That was the first crack in the glossy image of the company he had admired. By the end of the day, the phrase "Recommended place to work" already sounded hollow as Prithvi wondered who certifies such certifying bodies.

He returned home that night in a fog, the phrases echoing through his mind. Realignment. New direction. Fresh perspective. It all sounded like someone had hurled a blanket of corporate jargon over what was really unchecked gossip.

For a week, he dismissed it. He reminded himself that new jobs come with awkward beginnings, that he could make this work as well. Something within him kept changing. The new office was the same firm that he had admired, but it felt like another universe. Polite faces, plastic smiles, strained small talk. Work was done, but without trust, everything was meaningless, like actors playing efficiency. When he requested fundamental resources, approvals wandered from one office to another. Everyone was busy avoiding blame. Meetings were more about defending turf than solving problems.

He came to understand, slowly and painfully, that the true transfer was not that of the employee he had replaced, but the conscience of the company had been transferred elsewhere a long time ago. What he was dealing with now was not one bad decision; it was a trend of an establishment that accepted wrong as long as it was convenient. He had witnessed politics in the past, but this was different. This was professionalism dressed up in apathy.

One day, eating alone in the cafeteria, he caught two top managers discussing another worker's unexpected reassignment. They joked about it, labelling it "a minor shuffle." The fellow they were discussing had a baby just born at home and had recently signed a lease on a house nearer the old office. Hearing their laughter, something hardened secretly within him. He made up his mind then that he would never allow this to be his routine.

Towards the end of the week, he filed his resignation. The easiest and the hardest at the same time. He lacked a contingency plan, no follow-up strategy on his mind, but a feeling that staying in a place that denied dignity was more dangerous than the unknown.

He was no longer annoyed; he was merely thoughtful. Justice does not eradicate at once; it oozes out, in habits, in trifles, until it becomes commonplace that people are inconsequential components.

That night, on his way out, taking his last box, he promised himself at least, next time he founded or ran a team, its foundation would not be performance or market share or ambition. It would be culture, intentional, transparent, lived culture. The type that wouldn't allow a person to wake up one morning and discover his seat taken by surprise.

It took him some time to define what that looked like. Culture, of course, was that word everyone bandied about and really meant nothing. But to Prithvi, it was beginning to mean something, something tangible, the atmosphere between individuals. The unwritten agreement that holds you to see who looks over your shoulder or if you lie low at night. He hoped to build spaces where individuals did not need to interpret veiled meanings in e-mails or weigh each sentence on the scales of politics.

The ensuing months were surreal, professionally unclear, yet internally resolving. He took time to analyse every minor conduct he observed within that firm: how approvals proceeded with greater speed for the sycophants, how disagreement was penalised not directly but with ostracism, and how fear was used as a management technique. He analysed all these as a scientist analyses a failed experiment, questioning what design flaw had made this possible.

He understood that poor culture isn't created by poor people; it's created by neglect. It's what occurs when leaders confuse comfort with culture, when they tolerate small wrongs in exchange for the discomfort of addressing them. When that becomes a pattern, mediocrity masquerades as normalcy. The gossip that hurt him was only a symptom; the disease ran deeper.

It's ironic how life assigns significance to humiliation after the fact. What had seemed like unfairness then was beginning to resemble initiation. If not for that hurt, he would never have realised what finally shatters teams, not lack of talent or motivation, but the corrosive quiet of distrust. The transfer that he had witnessed, which made him question the conscience of the company he had so admired, ultimately defined his future leadership.

He began to see culture all around, in the way a senior spoke to a junior, in the way meetings concluded, in the way credit was given or denied. The most subtle signals conveyed the most profound realities. Some firms had lofty mission statements, but their hallways spoke of fear. Others were disorganised on paper but vibrant in essence, individuals debating openly, laughing openly, taking blame. He liked the messy integrity better than the slick deceit.

Gradually, a pattern unfolded: wherever individuals felt empowered to share their voice, creativity emerged. Wherever hierarchy insisted on deference, ability quietly dropped out. Those companies that succeeded didn't necessarily own the best technology or the biggest budgets; they just had clarity. Clarity about what type of behaviour was fostered and what wasn't. That clarity was cultivated by design.

Years down the line, when others would inquire of him why he was being so finicky about cultural congruence, he would smile and reply, "Because I've seen what happens when you leave it to chance." But at the time, in those initial months following his new job, it was not so much philosophy as a matter of survival, a resistance to allowing himself to become numb like the others whom he had left behind.

At home, he would replay the events of that day not to feel sorry for himself, but to examine how such a choice could go so many layers of approval before someone questioned how fair it was. He understood that most organisations do not operate by rules but culture; rules are codified, but culture determines when they're enforced. In this company, there were rules; fairness didn't exist.

That difference stayed with him. It made him think that culture couldn't be borrowed; it needed to be constructed, one unambiguous decision at a time.

He didn't yet know how he would do that. He only knew why he had to.

With the next assignment that came his way, Prithvi was still cautious a bit, not because he feared failure, but because he feared indifference. He vowed to himself that this time he would not let things go with the rationale of "that's how it's done here." He joined unobtrusively, listened more than he talked. In a matter of months, he already knew which undertows defined the company, who actually made the decisions, who got heard, and who got ignored. He hadn't yet spoken of culture with anyone, but he had begun to do something new: he was building it quietly, in the small choices most people regarded as mundane.

When he assembled his crew, he took an unconventional approach. On their first day, he didn't present them with the standard orientation booklet of slick slides on the company's mission and values. He gave them a plain card instead.

At the top, it read, "The kind of company we want to be."

Below it were five brief, handwritten lines, principles, not policies. He wrote them in his own words, simple and rough, but they mattered because they were personal.

They referred to it as the pledge card. Later, everyone in the department would own one, but initially, it was only his little experiment with bringing culture to light. Every individual was asked to write down one line in their own handwriting regarding how they envisioned their role playing a part in that notion. The exercise felt symbolic, but something changed in the room that day. For the first time, individuals weren't attempting to appease HR with rehearsed slogans; they were speaking what they actually believed.

That became the de facto mantra of his team. People were encouraged to gather and read out their pledge card, as the first thing every morning after arriving at work. And gradually, word got around. When new recruits reported to work, someone would slip them the pledge card even before HR could get to them.

But Prithvi's fixation on design did not stop at symbols. He had survived the havoc of nebulous hierarchies and nepotism, and he did not wish his new workplace to continue those habits.

He would not allow any department, not sales, not operations, not HR, to ever be more special than another. The initial months were rowdy; folks were not accustomed to equality being enforced so literally. At most firms, there are some departments that are the "heart" of things and others that become ghost arteries, unseen and without credit. Prithvi wouldn't allow that imbalance.

He did something unexpected: at the quarterly meeting and annual event, the limelight would not shine on one department's success story. Rather, the presentation was reworked into what he referred to as "Walk the mile." Each department gave one tale of how another department helped them to succeed.

Sales described how the service group had rescued a client relationship. HR described how finance had expedited reimbursement for a stranded technologist. Gradually, the atmosphere of celebration, from "look what I did," changed to "look what we did together."

The effect was subtle but real. People began noticing others' challenges. One young designer told Prithvi that she'd never understood how much pressure the procurement team was under until she spent a week following them around. That was another intentional exercise; each quarter, he had employees spend at least a week in a department they didn't know anything about. Engineers spent time alongside client support, salespeople spent hours on the shop floor, and accountants attended R&D review sessions. The aim was straightforward: empathy by exposure.

It wasn't always easy. People complained at first, telling them they didn't have time for "observation tours." But after a few cycles, it started changing talk. When departments really got it, what others went through, they quit blaming and began working together. The finger-pointing diminished. Requests clarified. Tone improved. It wasn't magic, it was design.

For Prithvi, this cross-department empathy was personal. He recalled how misunderstandings had become accusations back in his previous company because nobody took the time to look at the other person's point of view. He wanted to get rid of that blindness by building frameworks that compelled people to look.

It was about this time that he began to reconsider the company's induction process. He did not buy the idea of having bright individuals arrive on their first day and being subjected to policy manuals and boring slide presentations. He thought back to his own first day at one such company, sitting in a conference room hearing jargon he didn't relate to. He didn't want it for others.

So, he shifted the induction from a monologue to an experience. No PowerPoints for new hires, but instead time on the floor to see the rhythm of work. They sat with the individuals who fixed machines, took client calls, and drove delivery vans. Lunch on the first day was compulsory; everyone shared lunch, including Prithvi, not in a boardroom but at the same tables as the rest.

At lunch, he'd invite new members to discuss something personal, the origin story of their first paycheck, or what they envisioned doing outside of work. That little ceremony transformed strangers into co-workers in a matter of hours.

He thought culture was constructed not in meetings but in moments such as these.

But even as he worked on these gestures, Prithvi was aware that the greatest test of culture was communication. He had watched how jargon acts as a wall, a witty shield behind which ignorance hides. Despite studying in most elite business schools himself, wherein he had learnt all the jargon of management, he prohibited the internal use of jargon. He did not care if a person was aware of the latest management shorthand; what he cared about was whether he could articulate an idea in simple, earthy words.

He still vividly remembered the first time he encountered terms like Six Sigma, Kanban, 5S, JIT, TQM, and TPM, how overwhelmed he had felt, and how ignorant he believed himself to be. The feeling drove him to buy book after book, determined to learn.

Many weekends slipped by with him buried in those pages, so engrossed that Kiran, his wife, who had chosen to be a homemaker, often grew upset at the time he spent reading. One evening, after he had finished the books, she asked him to explain what he had learned.

As he spoke, breaking down each concept in simple terms, she listened patiently. When he was done, she smiled and said, "Why do you need books for this? Don't you think I follow all of these every day while running the house?"

Prithvi realised she was right. No one understood these principles better than housewives, who, unaware of the terms, quietly practiced every one of them, often at a black-belt level, without ever using those to make their 'housewife resume' look rosy.

When interviewing candidates, he would throw in questions that stripped away technical glamour. "Explain this to me like you're talking to a kid," he'd say. Many stumbled, trying to remember textbook definitions. The ones who could explain without buzzwords, simply and confidently, were the ones he would shortlist. For him, simplicity was intelligence made visible.

He also ensured, all communications had to be actionable, quantifiable, and closed-ended. For him, words as "ASAP" or "at the earliest" carried no meaning.

Each commitment was required to have a timeline attached, even if it meant that you had to say "by 6 PM Friday" rather than "soon."

This little discipline transformed the way groups operated. It eliminated the guesswork. When you make commitments measurable, responsibility becomes simple, and equity becomes automatic.

And because he believed culture had to extend beyond function, he ensured it was bias-free in every possible way.

Regional and religious biases were inconceivable to him.

At an internal gathering, someone casually joked that there weren't "enough people from our religion" in the company. Most people brushed it off, but Prithvi paused the meeting.

He reminded everyone that anything pertaining to culture can't be taken lightly. Then he asked the person to recommend a better employee selection process, so his concern would be addressed. The room went quiet, and the person realised the weight of what he'd said because he knew that the company followed a multi-level online assessment test before onboarding anyone to the company.

Prithvi didn't leave it there. He explained why the company never hosted religious celebrations on its premises.

India, as a country, has countless faiths and traditions, and even with the best intentions, someone could still end up feeling excluded. Anything that could divide people, even unintentionally, had no place in the workplace. And that included comments about identity, too.

He kept a calm tone, but there was a quiet authority in his voice - the kind of authority that only comes from having the moral high ground.

As a young professional, he learned what happens when leaders accept even the smallest prejudices. They grew unobtrusively, forming intangible cracks. And so now, he was adamant about preventing those cracks from ever taking hold.

It was not always smooth. Some opposed his insistence on justice. There were top managers who grumbled that the new system "made everyone too sensitive." But Prithvi did not budge.

"If you believe fairness to be over-sensitivity," he said to one of them, "then you've likely never been on the unfair side."

It was in many respects an exercise in the balance between idealism and pragmatism. He was not attempting to construct a utopia; he simply wanted decency made routine. The buildings, the pledge card, the cross-department rotations, and the rules of clear communication were his efforts to insulate fairness from degradation.

He did not want goodness to be mood-dependent. He wanted it to be institutional.

As his thoughts began to germinate, something started to change in the company's vibe. Meetings were more candid. Individuals took responsibility for holdups without hesitation. HR ceased being a repressive power and turned into an authentic support function. There was again laughter within the corridors, not nervous laughter, but relaxed laughter of individuals who feel secure.

When he glanced around one day at a company offsite, observing teams from various functions laughing together at a ridiculous game, he felt almost proud, not the self-serving kind, but the satisfaction of having created a space where people did not have to put on an act.

It was the first time that he really believed it could be done, that culture could be designed on purpose, that one could select behaviours with as much care as one selects a strategy.

He never spoke of it in public. No boisterous announcements, no culture campaigns. But the people he worked with noticed. The mood was more relaxed, the sense of trust deeper. Even though disputes were pure, people could yell at each other in a meeting and have lunch afterwards.

The transformation was imperceptible to the outside world, but to those who experienced it, it was everything.

And inside, Prithvi knew why it was so important. It wasn't about improved results or content workers.

And at last, he was conscious that he was moving in the right direction.

One thing was to plan culture on paper, and another was to observe it being experimented with in the midst of real work.

The first test arrived quietly, dressed up as a small dispute between two departments, operations and sales. The sales department had guaranteed a delivery timeline to a big client that the operations department could never achieve. When the postponement happened, fingers pointed, tempers flared, and emails began flying with passive-aggressive undertones.

In Prithvi's previous organisations, these kinds of scenarios took their predictable course, blame, defensiveness, and silence until a leader made a judgment in one's favour, generally inclined towards sales. People termed fights between Sales and Operations as natural and routine.

But for Prithvi, this wasn't the right thing, hence the need to be corrected. He drew these two parties into one room, and made them sit face by face, and began with not figures, but with compassion. "I want to know what you were up to," he said to the salesperson.

The salesperson was hesitant as he expected the chastisement, but the voice of Prithvi was even.

"I simply didn't want the client to lose trust," he replied at length. "I thought we could sort it out between us later."

Next, Prithvi addressed the operations lead. "And what is your biggest problem?"

She responded, "We never say no. We just keep getting stuck between promises and possibilities."

That's when he made a statement that the room remembered for months. "If a client's trust hinges on our people deceiving truth from one another, then we are constructing loyalty upon lies."

There was silence. Not silence that is awkward, but silence that is reflective, sparked by looking in the mirror moment. He did not yell, he did not chastise.

He instead had both teams make a chart of their process on the white board, from the moment the client committed to the moment we closed the last hand-off, highlighting every phase they went from fact to assumption. At the end of that exercise, everyone could see that the actual problem wasn't laziness or ego, it was a lack of mutual visibility.

Then, he created a single group email that included the operations manager, production planner, demand manager, and the sales team, ensuring everyone stayed in the same approval loop before committing anything to a client.

The rule sounded almost too simple, but the impact was immediate. Within weeks, communication became clearer, timelines became realistic, and client satisfaction started rising on its own. Later, when a strong ERP system was rolled out, this very practice was built into the software, making the process even tighter and more efficient.

But the greater victory was emotional. Departments that had competed began to work together. The phrase "they" gradually fell out of use in discussions and gave way to "we."

That's when Prithvi understood that culture wasn't tested in values workshops; it was tested in conflict.

And there were many more tests ahead.

One afternoon, a young technician came to him, visibly shaken. He had made a mistake on-site that caused a client complaint, and the regional sales head had already recommended termination because the mistake was big enough to cost the client a huge sum. The technician, barely in his twenties, stood outside Prithvi's office, voice trembling as he explained what had happened. It wasn't negligence, it was inexperience, a lapse born of fatigue and lack of guidance.

Most of the leaders would have endorsed the dismissal letter without a second thought; rather easier to make an example than to look into the failure of the system. But Prithvi noticed something different: the fear in the boy's eyes. The fear of being discarded due to one wrong.

He requested the service log, followed the chain, and found that the young man had indeed reported a warning signal two days previously, only to see his message get lost among the flurry of other work. The mistake was not a one-off; it was systemic.

Instead of firing him, Prithvi did something unexpected: he called the entire service team for a short meeting and began by saying, "We're not here to assign blame. We're here to understand how good people end up making avoidable mistakes."

The technician was requested to take everyone through his side of things. By its end, the team was not staring at him as the issue any longer, but at the process. For many, it was the first time that they saw how one overlooked nod, one unclear command, one hurried message had snowballed into a crisis.

The team agreed on a simple new checklist before closing any job. Prithvi made it clear that this would stay only for six months. He believed that most inefficiencies come from gaps in culture, not from the absence of procedures, and piling on more rules only breeds bureaucracy. In his view, an honest mistake born out of inexperience shouldn't automatically become the reason for a permanent new process.

And, in a low-key but significant move, the technician not only stayed on but was also directly mentored by a senior manager for the subsequent six months.

One decision sent shockwaves through the firm. News flashed that Prithvi didn't fire for incompetence; he fired for integrity, not for mistakes. The workforce ceased concealing errors, started flagging problems in advance, and the whole system was more transparent.

It was yet another lesson that would remain with him: culture blooms most strongly when individuals feel free to speak the truth.

There were other instances, too, low-key but equally defining.

One senior manager had attempted to pull rank in an internal project meeting, claiming that sales targets created a justification for "special treatment" for his team. Prithvi listened attentively and then remarked, "Let me ask you something: when a client's call gets ignored, do they say 'the sales department didn't respond,' or do they say 'the company didn't respond'?"

The supervisor looked embarrassed but got it. Prithvi didn't have to yell. The hierarchy didn't disappear overnight, but as time went by, people started to pick up on the notion that respect wasn't a department-based or title-based thing; it was based on behaviour.

Culture, he had come to believe, was about protecting that invisible connection, the one that holds people together even when opinions differ.

Eventually, even recruits could sense that. At induction, Prithvi took care that none of them felt overawed by names. When he joined them at lunch on their very first day, they tended to assume that he was yet another middle-level manager until someone nudged them and told them he was the company head. His presence at the lunch table was not a publicity stunt; he indicated that leadership was not remoteness.

He also asked leaders to speak in plain language. One day, at a quarterly review, one of the newly appointed senior executives began his presentation full of dense management lingo, "strategic bandwidth allocation," "performance verticals," and "resource optimisation metrics." Prithvi allowed him to complete his presentation, then smiled and said, "Can you explain all that to a seventh grader?"

The man stammered and laughed, then attempted again, this time explaining the real work in simple terms. The room lit up. From that moment forward, presentations throughout the company became clearer, brighter, and more human.

His aversion to jargon was not about style; it was about genuineness. He used to say that individuals hide behind convoluted words when they are not sure about clarity. "If we cannot explain what we do, clearly," he would utter, "perhaps we are not doing it clearly either."

Then came the true test, the kind that shows whether culture is superficial or substantial.

A top HR executive, a woman who had been with the organisation for some time and apparently was known to have adapted to company culture, got caught subtly giving preference to candidates from her own community during hiring. It wasn't overt discrimination, yet habits don't deceive. She justified it when confronted, claiming it helped with "comfort and retention."

Prithvi didn't need to think about it. He had invested decades creating a workplace in which equality was not an option. He explained to her in kind but firm terms that comfort founded on bias was an illness, not an approach. She departed the business shortly afterwards, and her departure broadcast a message loud and clear: this culture made no exceptions for convenience.

But even in difficult decisions, he never let go of compassion. In a situation where an aged housekeeping member was discovered to have taken money from the cash vault, which was always kept open, not because of greed, but due to his financial crisis, Prithvi resolved to handle this without much ado. The cash was reclaimed, but the man was not disgraced publicly. Discipline without dignity is, however, merely punishment, as he realised later, explaining this to his management team. The moral was this: get everyone responsible, but never put them down.

Another powerful incident that sent a strong message across the organisation is one that the CFO still recalls with some embarrassment.

"This was when we had become a sizeable company and were required to spend 2% of our profits on CSR activities as per the government mandate. I approached Prithvi to share my idea of partnering with an NGO that worked in the slums of Chennai."

Prithvi, however, was unaware of the formal concept of CSR. He listened patiently and then said, "We already mould people into ethical, humane individuals. Local villagers freely walk into our gateless facility to collect drinking water for their households. We pay the caterer for lunch for 350 people every day, even though we have just over 200 employees, because villagers, courier staff, and truck drivers visiting the industrial township see our facility as a place where they can eat for free without being questioned. What better CSR can we do?"

"None of these qualify as CSR," I had replied.

Prithvi fell silent for a moment. Then he said, "Go ahead. But partner only with agencies that do not display pictures of the poorest, most helpless-looking slum children on their websites while seeking donations. I have a problem with such organisations that use close-up images of such innocent children in the public domain. It often feels like those images are used more for vested interest to market the organisation than to support the genuine cause."

The CFO continued, "I knew what he meant by this because, once, he had not allowed any of us to participate in a marathon event titled *"Run for the Girl Child"* as his friend was the event organiser, and Prithvi knew that this friend had aborted his own girl child. Prithvi always asked us to stay away from such people who take undue advantage of something as pure as human emotion.

Even after two months of searching, we couldn't find an agency that met Prithvi's guidelines. However, during this process, we came across an old-age home that was on the verge of shutting down. A woman had started it years ago, but after she passed away, her daughter was struggling to keep it running while managing her own family and job."

"Prithvi immediately approved the idea of adopting the old-age home. We renovated the entire building, replaced furniture and upholstery, and our employees voluntarily contributed daily essentials from their own salaries."

"The smiles on the faces of the elderly when we invited them as chief guests to hoist the flag at our facility on Independence Day, and the joy our people felt in giving, were priceless. It meant far more to us than fulfilling a CSR mandate."

"We made sure none of this ever appeared on our website or in the public domain, honouring Prithvi's principles."

Prithvi realised something that night, culture wasn't so much what you constructed; it was what you rejected becoming.

And the business he was constructing had begun to reflect that rejection.

Nevertheless, he knew that culture wasn't a point of arrival. It required tending, reinforcement, and incessant narrative. Because individuals forgot. Success bred complacency. So he set about implementing rituals to preserve the memory, small ones, significant ones.

Each morning stand-up meeting started with an individual reading out their line from the pledge card. Not as a rule, but as a reminder. Leaders shared one experience each quarter that challenged their values and what they did about it. It established a culture in which errors were considered learning materials, not proof of judgment.

Piece by piece, the culture became self-enforcing. When a violation occurred, peers called them on it before leadership was required to. When a person exemplified it, thanks came from everywhere. That was the true success: a culture that no longer relied on enforcement, because it had become second nature.

And in that moment of instinct, Prithvi realised his life's silent redemption, evidence that out of witnessing an unjust replacement, an entire philosophy of justice was born.

Years later, when the company had grown to a few thousand people and its name began appearing in industry circles, Prithvi found himself in a familiar but eerily inverted situation. One of his senior managers had become the subject of internal complaints. Some people accused him of being arrogant, of taking credit for others' work, of playing politics.

The HR team, wary, recommended shifting the man to another vertical "for a while," simply to keep the lid on things. It was precisely the sort of temporary fix Prithvi had once witnessed in one of his jobs, tidy on paper, unjust in spirit. He sat through this in silence, his hands folded, as the team talked possibilities. Then, after a long pause, he spoke quietly, "Transfers don't solve culture. They merely move the issue."

The room went silent. Everyone understood this was personal.

The following morning, he summoned a meeting, not only with HR, but with the targeted manager and the complainants. Everyone anticipated a fight, but Prithvi had other plans. He requested that everyone tell him the exact thing that had created the discomfort without using any adjectives or giving any opinions, and instead, stating only facts. And then he addressed the manager and said, "You will get to respond after everyone has had a chance to talk. But for now, I want you to listen without defending."

It was uncomfortable to start with. Accusations were made, and then toned down into remarks. Some were overhyped, some were real. When his turn came, the manager hesitated, acknowledging that he'd overpressed in pursuit of outcomes, not infrequently forgetting people had feelings, not targets. He wasn't sinister, just oblivious.

Prithvi nodded. "We'll treat this as a course correction, not a trial."

He assigned the man to a mentor who was a senior leader known for emotional intelligence and asked him to co-lead a people development initiative for six months. It was not a punishment, not any scapegoating either; it was just accountability with dignity.

A few months on, one afternoon, when Prithvi saw the same group that had previously complained about him enjoying lunch together with him, he smiled because culture had done what it was meant to, with fairness, consideration, and grace.

He passed through the long corridor that day that led to the HR department. The glass cubicles were light now, with inclusion, respect, and clarity posters on them. It hit him that the corridor was unlike the one he had passed through many years before, when he was witnessing an employee being transferred unjustly. But that sense of that day stayed with him, shaping every impulse he'd taken since.

The philosophy that had previously lingered in his personal memo had now become the identity of the company. The pledge card had escalated to a complete internal charter, distributed to every new joiner, every leader had to update it, and every year saw small changes that embraced the growth of the company. The line at the top remained constant: "The kind of company we want to be."

It wasn't a statement any longer. It was muscle memory.

The more he pondered, the more he was sure that creating culture wasn't perfecting. It was creating enough truth so that imperfection could be seen without embarrassment. He didn't want everyone to become ideals each day, but he wanted an environment where it was impossible to conceal when they weren't.

During one leadership session, someone once asked him half-jokingly, "If culture is everything, what's left for strategy?"

He chuckled. "Strategy creates the game plan," he replied. "Culture determines whether or not people will believe in it long enough to make it happen."

Prithvi also learned, over time, that culture was self-curing when cultivated correctly. If you seed clarity and fairness deep enough, the organisation begins fixing itself without your needing to get involved. He witnessed teams fixing problems without it going up the chain, leaders stepping up and taking accountability, and people raising moral red flags before HR ever got in on it.

Those instances filled him with great satisfaction, not because they lightened his work, but because they showed that trust, once it is gained, grows secretly.

As the firm expanded and fresh faces occupied the corridors, Prithvi gradually stepped back from day-to-day work. He wanted culture to endure after he was gone, to be in place even when he wasn't around. So he began mentoring a next-generation crop of leaders, not teaching them processes, but principles.

Years later, when he reflected on his path, he couldn't recall the awards or profits as clearly as he recalled faces, people who had remained, people who had grown, people who had discovered their voice under his guidance, and the kids of employees achieving their career aspirations under Prithvi's mentorship. All of them, in some capacity, were testament that fairness could be scaled, that humanity and success need not be adversaries.

He had once mentioned that he wanted to start a company where nobody was afraid of being honest. And now, as he looked at his topmost leaders guiding others with the same credo, he knew that he had done something more than just building a business; he had created an ecosystem of trust.

Later that evening, walking through the office for a final time before departure, he passed by the wall where the original version of the pledge card was still hung in a frame. The edges were worn, the ink a bit smudged, but the message was clear. He smiled inwardly, gently touched it, and whispered, nearly to himself, "By design, not default."

The journey that had begun with discomfort and disbelief had concluded in quiet purpose.

And in this instant, he experienced a stillness of peace, the kind that appears when the circle of sorrow had at last become purpose.

Conclusion

Looking back at myself as I have gone through, I often ask myself just how much the world of work, and leadership in particular, has changed, and how much it hasn't changed. Technology has changed, systems have evolved, industries have re-invented themselves half a dozen times over, yet the basic fabric of what holds an organisation together remains the same: trust, compassion, and purpose.

I have always held that work leadership is not much different from parenting at home. The more years pass, the more this view is strengthened. In my view, both are about raising people, making them feel they belong, and empowering them to find out their potential. We don't view our children as cost centres; we view them as possibilities. The same applies to employees. When leaders cease perceiving their team members as "resources" and begin viewing them as an extension of their own family members, something transformational occurs; loyalty and performance become second nature.

Throughout my years of leading teams around geographies, I have witnessed one given truth: people don't stay for wage or brand name; they stay for culture. Culture determines everything: how people make decisions, how disputes are settled, how errors are handled. And the more leaders attempt to exert control, the less trusting they become.

As I started constructing my leadership philosophy, I wished to create a culture of fearlessness, love, and affection, a place that would feel like coming home. I wanted to create a community where individuals exclaimed "Thank God it's Monday" just as readily as they exclaimed "Thank God it's Friday."

Gradually, that vision materialised in ways I could never have foreseen. From twenty-two to thousands, from doubts to sustainability, we expanded not because of policy but because of the culture that united us.

But I fear what I observe of the contemporary business world. The post-pandemic world has celebrated convenience at the expense of connection. The "Work from Home" culture, though ostensibly convenient, from my perspective, is robbing the human spirit that flourishes in the midst of a company in many ways. We are seeing a gradual erosion of camaraderie. People no longer gather over coffee, brainstorm in corridors, or giggle over dumb blunders. In families as well, we have transitioned from joint families to nuclear ones and now to single living. Every member of the same home is isolated to their own screen. And then the companies join in on this loneliness by offering remote work as an advantage.

I fear that loneliness is the next epidemic. Offices were once rich ecosystems of energy, emotion, and exchange, truly defining what is called an Organisation; now they are on the verge of becoming transactional screens with stifled faces.

In the interest of flexibility and productivity, we are raising a generation that will be efficient but not empathetic. Sooner or later, I feel, companies that rely heavily on remote work will realise the cost of it. A few decades down the line, they may struggle to find capable successors simply because their future leaders never spent enough time in-person dealing with people and never learned how to nurture or develop them.

I think that current leaders like us need to turn this tide around. If commute time to work is an issue, let us shorten the distance between work and home. Let us cluster offices and communities together, rather than offices within cities. We should not allow efficiency to become a substitute for humanity. It's all about doing the right thing, regardless.

The other area that I believe we should develop is in the way we treat the young generation. I have heard some of the senior leaders complain, these millennials are not going to work. But I don't consider them lazy. I see every generation as more expressive, independent, and fearless than the one before, and this generation is no different. They ask questions; they want to understand the *why* behind every *what.* It's not rebellion, it's awareness. I've noticed it with young colleagues: they won't follow rules that don't make sense. I think they deserve respect for that mindset.

The world needs those who question conventions, not those who blindly obey. Regardless of generation, when we show people the value behind the work and what's in it for them, they align naturally and remain loyal for the long term.

Leadership now needs to adapt to understand that motivation is no longer based on authority, but alignment. Simply setting a vision isn't sufficient; we need to relate it to each person's purpose. Treat each decision as if you are making it about your own child. When you frame it that way, even the most difficult business decisions become easy.

Over time, I also came to realize that a team's true strength lies as much at the bottom as it does at the top.

It's the frontline people, the ones who work as hard, who create, build, and deliver, who form the backbone of any organization, yet are often the most overlooked. To me, it's like a head thinking it's bigger than the legs that carry it.

If I have one message, I want to leave with all the readers of this book, it is this: create your own *MahiWay.* Don't emulate anyone. Construct your definition of truth, love, and logic that resonates with you. Be true to yourself. Be you.

After three decades of work, one lesson stands out: if you want a business to endure across generations, culture has to come before profit. It has to be absolute, with no exceptions, no matter how minor the breach seems or how senior the person involved is. The irony is that once you make culture truly non-negotiable, the rest follows almost effortlessly. Revenue grows, cash flow strengthens, operations become leaner, and profits rise on their own. And to top that all, the business will last for generations.

That, to me, is the true test of leadership.

Mahiway…Closing Comment

Thank you for choosing to spend your time and money on this book.

As one leads an enterprise, one encounters continual challenges, opportunities, and learnings across every department of the organisation. Including them all would have made the book excessively bulky.

In this book, I have therefore provided you with a summary of *'what'* and *'how'* of The *Mahiway.*

If any part of the book resonated and you'd like to ask something more in detail, feel free to write to me at -

2025mahiway@gmail.com.

I'll do my best to respond over the weekends or on as & when basis.

Cheers!

Verses Kindler Publication

Reach us through our website -

https://www.verseskindlerpublication.com/

For more information visit our

Instagram or Facebook page.